friendship
and
community

First published 2002

Published by:
North West Training and Development Team
Adamson House, Pomona Strand
Old Trafford, Manchester, M16 0BA
Tel: 0161 877 7499

The authors would like to thank the following for their stories and support: Ark Housing Association service users and staff; Alan Barr; Peter Bates; Julia Champion; Owen Cooper; Sylvia Crick; Jenny Flowerdew; Jane Gray and Edinburgh Development Group; Linda Headland and Lesley Whiteside; Monica Hunter; Chris Jones; Kristjana Kristiannsen; Kirsten, Sylvia and Alister Lawrie; Alan Lewis; Michelle Livesley; Catriona May; Mhairi McAughtrie; Moira McDonald; Kay Mills; John O'Brien; John Redwood and Inclusion Alliance; David Robertson and Stirling and Alloa LETS; Scott Simpson; Tracy Paterson; Michelle Thomson; Fiona Wallace; Jan Wallace; Liza Ware; and Duncan Yates.

Design and typesetting by Cluny Sheeler
Illustrations by Jon Harker
Printed and bound by Scotprint, Haddington, East Lothian, Scotland.

A CIP record is available from the British Library
ISBN: 1 8983 8503 3

friendship
and
community

practical strategies for making connections in communities

jo kennedy   *helen sanderson*   *helen wilson*

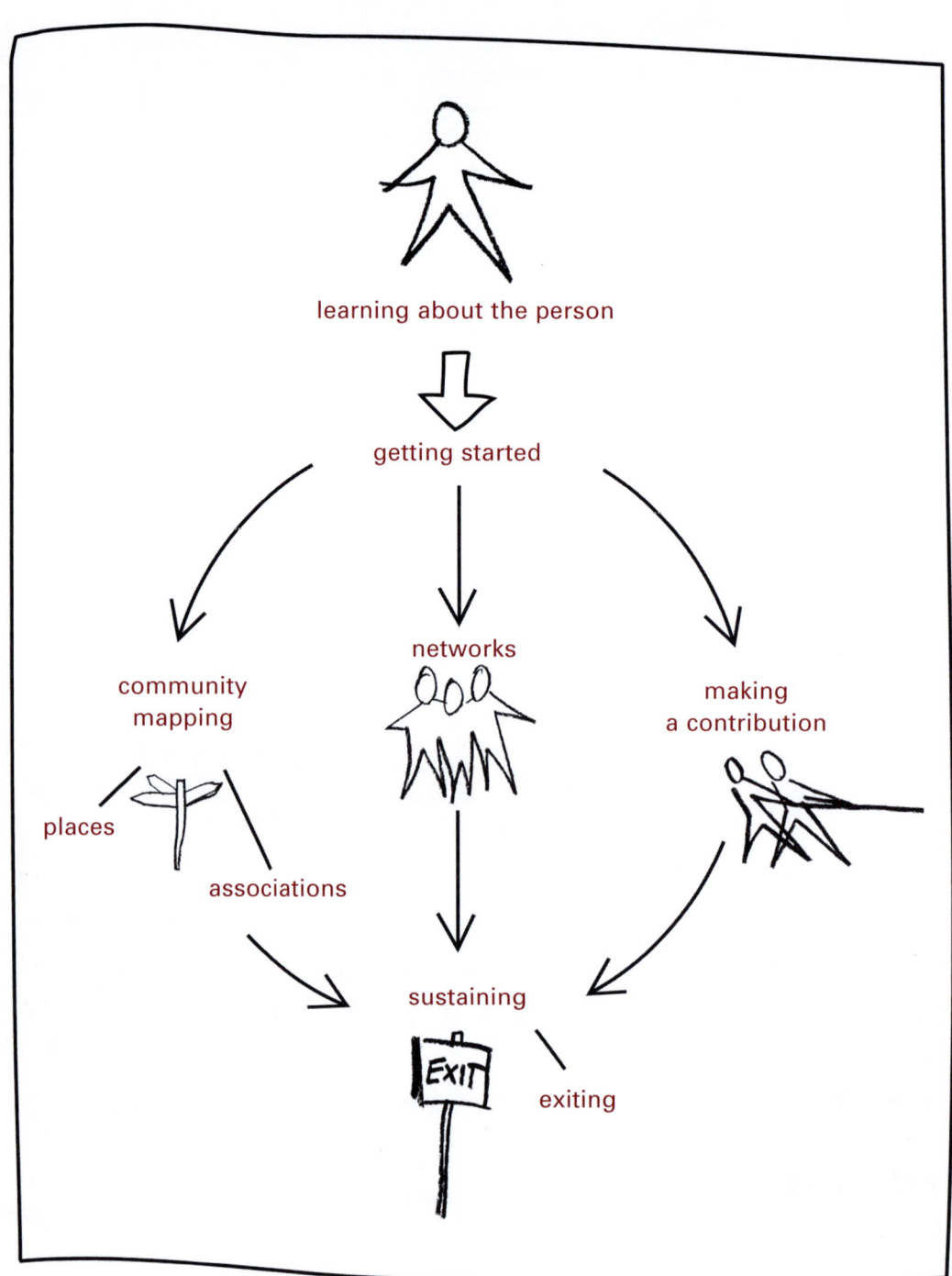

learning about the person

getting started

community
mapping

networks

making
a contribution

places

associations

sustaining

EXIT

exiting

The community connecting approach

contents ——————————————————

I think it is good to have a book about this because it is the real world. If there were no friends in the world people would be on their own. The world is friends and it's people. I would like there to be more people to encourage people to make friends.

Monica Hunter
People First, Scotland

Despite the undoubted progress that has been made by public services in improving the lives of people with learning disabilities, one aspect stands out as being very much the same. People with learning disabilities are, on the whole, still not part of their local communities in terms of the relationships and connections that many non-disabled people take for granted. For those of us brought up on John O'Brien's 'Five Accomplishments', the challenge of community participation is the one where we have singularly failed.

Perhaps one of the main causes of this is to be found in my first sentence. We have tended to see it as the responsibility of 'public services' to help people be part of their communities. Yet those public services are perhaps the least well placed to achieve this – particularly if driven from a traditional social services perspective. Being part of one's community and being genuinely connected with other people arises through the contacts and relationships that we develop in everyday life. If those relationships are circumscribed by 'services' then the extent to which we become part of our communities will be similarly limited.

In reflecting back on when I moved house a few years ago, my community connections occurred because of roles I possess that we often deny to people with learning disabilities. The new house (householder role) had locks missing, so we got to know Mike, hardware store owner and pillar of the local community.

He introduced us to John, a handyman who knew everyone in the area. This linked us into Stephanie, who became our cleaner. Meanwhile through our son (parental role) we met several new friends, and through them Matthew, who became our babysitter. At work (employee role) we made friends in the community which supplemented old friends from years ago (student role) who lived nearby. And so on ... Community connections are about services facilitating and then letting go – not about taking responsibility for peoples' lives.

As we work to deliver Valuing People, this is one of the greatest challenges. Traditional service approaches often deny people the opportunity to be householders, parents, employees and students and thus restrict community connections. The people who can make the greatest impact in the lives of people with learning disabilities are other local citizens. Releasing that potential requires great changes in attitudes both from our communities and from professionals and public organizations. This book will, I am sure, make an important contribution towards this aspiration.

Rob Greig
Valuing People, Director of Implementation

introduction

Friendship is about hope: between friends we talk about our futures; our ideals and larger than life meanings.

Ray Pahl[1]

Community – our endless connections with responsibilities towards each other.

James Baldwin

This book is a response to the fact that many people, despite being thought of as 'living in-community', are in reality very isolated. Regardless of the political rhetoric, our society is failing to be inclusive, sometimes as a result of deliberate action, sometimes as a result of neglect or inefficiency. We hear constantly about the breakdown of community life and the social problems – rising crime, drug and alcohol abuse, higher rates of depression and suicide – that are a consequence. Some of this comes to us through the media, some through personal experience.

The breakdown of community has been attributed to factors such as an increase in commuting, greater numbers of working-women, and the concentration of poor housing and high unemployment rates in particular areas. At the same time as the widely reported breakdown of community, we have newcomers into

community. These include people with learning disabilities or mental health problems who have lived for many years in hospitals that have now closed down. They also include refugees and asylum seekers.

There is a growing nostalgia for the 'good old days' when people looked out for the other folk in their neighbourhood. This book is not harking back to such a past, mythical or otherwise. Instead it is seeking to find ways of making the communities that we do have more inclusive. Most of the stories found here focus on people with learning disabilities but the approaches we describe could benefit anyone who feels excluded, particularly those with mental health problems or physical disabilities.

The book is based on the learning and experience of many paid and unpaid people who are attempting to make our communities more accepting and inclusive places. We hope that it will be useful for anyone practically involved in this challenge.

How did we get here – Community Care?

The last 30 years have been marked by policies promoting community care, perhaps the most important of which was the NHS and Community Care Act (1990). Services supporting people with disabilities have changed considerably over this time and most people have moved out of hospital and are now supported in individual accommodation or group homes.[2]

These changes have been made for several reasons: a series of scandals in long-stay hospitals, research demonstrating the dehumanising effect of institutions,[3] and the adoption of the principles of normalisation and ordinary living.[4] It has also always been suspected by many that the prospect of financial savings through care in the community was a key factor in its adoption. Disabled people themselves have lobbied for change, redefining disability as social oppression and demanding access to mainstream housing and control of their own lives.[5] This has led to changes in policy such as the introduction of the Community Care (Direct Payments) Act (1996).

Throughout these changes there has been a widespread assumption that *'if a person has been discharged from a hospital site they are defined as living in the community'*, with all the 'benefits' in terms of opportunities for employment and friendship that that accrues.[6]

Being in the community, however, has frequently not led to friendships for people coming out of hospitals. Very few have reciprocal friendships[7] and most of their relationships are with other service users and staff.[8]

At the same time, it is evident that the principle aims of many people with disabilities include greater participation and the building of wider social networks.[9] Time and again, when people with disabilities are asked what they want, they say it is the chance to have an ordinary life with a job and friends in a place they choose to live. Yet still, people with disabilities are more isolated than other members of the community.

This isolation has been shown to lead to poorer health and even an increased risk of mortality.[10] Robert Putnam sums this up:

> As a rough rule of thumb, if you belong to no groups but decide to join one, you cut your risk of dying over the next year in half. If you smoke and belong to no groups, it's a toss-up statistically whether you should stop smoking or start joining.[11]

There are several explanations for why disabled people are more vulnerable to isolation than others:

- Movement – many people become more disabled as they get older and have to move out of their family homes into smaller houses or residential homes away from the community they have lived in for many years. In some cases this involves moving to another part of the country to be nearer relatives. Those with learning disabilities or mental health problems have often moved out of hospital into an entirely new community or one in which they have not lived for many years. Many people can end up in communities that are more convenient for support agencies than for the individuals themselves. For anyone, moving into a new geographical community requires the effort to meet new people.
- Prejudice and discrimination – commonly, disabled people are either perceived as redundant or viewed with suspicion. Stigma comes from our ignorance as a society about disability and from our fear and intolerance of difference. Disabled people often find themselves needing to overcome prejudicial attitudes on an individual basis before they can break into community.
- Segregation – many disabled people have been segregated in hospitals and day centres for most of their lives. Once closed down, residents lose the networks they developed there and are forced to build new networks

from scratch with little experience of developing relationships in the outside world.

Isolation is, then, frequently the result of exclusion:

> the perception that people with severe disabilities should live outside the boundary of membership. Inside the boundary, people may dislike or disapprove of one another, people may have conflicts, people may avoid one another, and people may let one another down. But within the boundary of acknowledged membership, people see one another as approximately equal, they see the possibility of mutuality, and they consider others entitled to fair treatment and a share in common resources.[12]

Over the last 20–30 years efforts have been made to overcome some of these boundaries. Normalisation[13] and the Five Accomplishments[14] have emphasised the rights of people with disabilities to live in ordinary places, take part in ordinary activities and develop relationships like everyone else. These principles have led to changes in the way disabled people are supported with more emphasis being placed on person centred planning[15] and supported living.[16]

At the same time, the disability movement has campaigned for equal rights for people with disabilities, defining the problem of exclusion as societal rather than individual.[17] These rights extend to the right to build friendships on equal terms and with anyone. There is often concern that disabled people are encouraged only to build friendships with non-disabled people (see Chapter One) but equal rights would seem to demand that *'Justice involves making friends, lots of friends, many kinds of friends … [friends who] empower one another to keep making change.'*[18]

Community connecting pioneers

Options in Community Living, in Madison, Options for Individuals Inc., in Louisville, Kentucky, and John McKnight, working in Chicago, have all been pioneers in community connecting in America. Each organisation has rooted its efforts firmly in person centred planning, working outwards from individual preferences to support disabled people to develop networks. John McKnight has adopted a community development approach, working with existing clubs and associations, supporting the development of groups designed to meet the needs of the whole community, and emphasising the contribution disabled people can make to their communities. Such pioneering work has been influential in both the USA and Britain, yet there is still remarkably little effective connecting within communities being undertaken by community care services.

Outside of services, Circles of Support have been instrumental both in sustaining individuals within their family and friendship networks and in rebuilding networks for people who have become isolated.

> Circle thinking is simply the philosophy of empowerment combined with a belief in the importance of natural community relationships.[19]

This work was started by Judith Snow, Jack Pearpoint and Marsha Forrest in Canada, and by Beth Mount in the USA. It has been developed throughout the UK by Circles Network. The triumphs and challenges of Circles of Support are described in Chapter Five.[20]

Policies

At the same time, the government's 'social inclusion' strategies, which apply to the general population, fail to emphasise the importance of including disabled people. Policy initiatives for disabled people are full of the rhetoric of inclusion, but 'inclusion' is ill-defined and little guidance is given on how to achieve it. Mainstream service development continues to exclude people with extra support needs and an ethos of segregation is reinforced. Disabled people are more likely to be affected by other social problems – poverty, poor housing and lack of opportunity – than the rest of the population and are therefore more affected by the success of government policies in tackling these generic issues.

*

In this book we focus specifically on what individuals, working for the most part within services, can do to support connecting within communities. Our belief is that change needs to occur at an individual, a community and a service level. Throughout the book we adopt the social model of disability, advocating that individuals are excluded not so much by their disability but by society's attitudes towards that disability. The book also explores ideas, gleaned from community development practice, that can be used to promote communities that are more inclusive to disabled people.

We acknowledge, reluctantly, that there is a limited amount individuals can do. The inclusion of disabled people in our society needs to be addressed more comprehensively at a policy level. Disabled people are also often poor, unemployed, badly housed and discriminated against because of their race or gender.

These issues lie beyond the scope of this book but addressing them is crucial if we are to achieve an inclusive society.

In writing this book we felt a sense of urgency, impelled by the loneliness experienced by many people excluded from community, and by the knowledge that having people who care for us gives meaning and richness to all our lives:

I believe there is a crack in the world – it is my job to keep people from falling down that crack.[21]

We were also keenly aware that excluding individuals from the mainstream of community life because of their disabilities actually leaves our communities impoverished.

> A true community is only able to grow and strengthen itself by including all of its members and finding room for them to develop their capacities within its own pattern of growth.[22]

To build community and develop networks we seek to:

* build an environment in which all individuals are able to contribute
* provide opportunities for connection between individuals who have something in common.

This book aims to provide practical ideas, raise issues, and share stories regarding what we are learning about how to encourage friendships and build community. We begin, in Chapter One, by grounding this in our understanding of what friendship and community mean. Building on individuals' preferences and using their gifts is a starting point for enabling friendships and strengthening communities. We suggest a range of ways of seeing our lives from different person-centred approaches. We call these approaches 'windows', and in Chapter Two describe how using them can give us a perspective on someone's life that reveals the real person – the person all too often obscured by labels and reputations.

With a clear and shared understanding of who the focus person is, we suggest, in Chapter Three, ways of discovering or developing opportunities to connect. One way to begin is by connecting through sharing places or joining associations. In Chapter Four we explore community mapping, and the notion of becoming a 'detective', following the leads that could result in opportunities and links.

Throughout the book we look at community building from different perspectives acknowledging that a variety of people can undertake it:

- individuals themselves
- friends and family
- a person employed as a community builder, who can provide an independent service to individuals
- a member of staff employed by a support agency as a community builder
- a member of staff in a keyworker or support role who takes on the role of community builder as a priority function of her job.

Whoever is taking the initiative, networks can be explored as another way to make connections. In Chapter Five we consider how using networks – the focus person's, your own, friends, families, or more formal trust networks – can provide opportunities for friendship.

Making a contribution is fundamental to citizenship and with this in mind Chapter Six examines different ways of contributing, from volunteering and work to LETS schemes and campaigning.

Throughout the book we share stories told by people themselves or their allies. There are stories of sparkling triumphs, of more modest successes, and of difficulties and lessons learned. Many of these stories provide pointers towards how we can support friendships over time. Chapter Seven summarises what we are learning about sustaining friendships and letting go.

Contributing to people developing friendships and being part of communities demands fundamental changes in organizations. In Chapter Eight we discuss the implications of this change for staff, managers, staff development and service design. Fundamentally, this change means that friendship and community are no longer seen as the icing on the cake. They are the cake – the core work of support services.

chapter one
friendship and community

It is impossible to over-emphasise the immense need men have to be really listened to, to be taken seriously, to be understood. No one can develop freely in this world and find a full life, without feeling understood by at least one person.

Paul Tournier

The isolation of many people with disabilities testifies to the fact that we cannot always expect individuals to overcome society's barriers by themselves. The hardest, most challenging, but ultimately most rewarding, work of those who support people with disabilities is a deliberate focus on building community with them and helping them to develop and sustain relationships.

Some people reject the notion that artificial interventions in the process of building community can ever be effective – friendships occur naturally or not at all. Deborah Reidy, whose work focuses on including people with disabilities in associational life, agrees, to some extent: '*Friendship is the indefinable spark between two people that cannot be fabricated with any amount of effort*'. However, she goes on to say, '*it is possible to create the conditions that encourage friendship to flourish*'.[23]

Before beginning to make connections within communities it is essential to set some parameters. So, in this introductory chapter, we offer some reflections on what defines community and what defines friendship.

WHAT DO WE MEAN BY COMMUNITY?

Remarkably, for a word that is constantly in use, there is no consensus on what we mean by community. There is, however, a consensus that society has lost a sense of 'community'. In *Bowling Alone* Robert Putnam describes this as a decline in 'social capital' or in the *'social networks and the norms of reciprocity and trustworthiness which arise from them'* – the connections among individuals.

What we are lacking is the psychological sense of community:

> There are times in a society when a myriad of social phenomena indicate that a particular human need is so seriously frustrated, with consequences sufficiently widespread and ominous, as to force us to give it special emphasis. We are living in such times. The young and the old; residents of any geographical area; the more or less educated; the political left, right and centre; the professional and the non-professional; the rich and the poor – within each of these groupings sizable numbers of people feel alone, unwanted, and unneeded; They may spend a large part of their time in densely populated settings, interacting with other people in a transient or sustained way, and yet be plagued by feelings of aloneness and the stabbing knowledge that physical proximity and psychological closeness can be amazingly unrelated.[24]

The sense that we have lost 'community' is endemic in society and does not only apply to people with disabilities. Putnam's message is that *'we desperately need an era of civic inventiveness to create a renewed set of institutions and channels for a reinvigorated civic life that will fit the way we have come to live'*. The message of this book is that one way to achieve this is to end the exclusion of disabled people and begin allowing them to make their contribution. On a wider level, *'perhaps one of the most important reasons to work on including individuals is the opportunity for community members to open their eyes and hearts'*.[25]

The definition of community might be divided into three parts: community as geography, community as a local social system, and community as shared identity. Here, we concentrate less on community as geography – although where an individual lives has been shown to be important in presenting opportunities to develop networks – and more on the latter definitions.[26]

When we speak of community we speak of belonging either to a neighbourhood, a network of family or friends, or to a community of shared interest. Seymour Saranson describes this as:

> the sense that one is part of a readily available, mutually supportive network of relationships upon which one could depend and as a result of which one did not experience sustained feelings of loneliness that impel one to actions or to adapting to a lifestyle ... masking anxiety and setting the stage for later more destructive anguish.[27]

WHAT DO WE MEAN BY FRIENDSHIP?

The Chambers English Dictionary defines a friend as '*one loving or attached to another: an intimate acquaintance: a favourer, well-wisher, supporter*'.

The term covers a whole spectrum of relationships from lover to simple acquaintance. The Ordinary Life Working Group defines the different ways people relate to each other as:

- friendship – having friends, relationships, including a 'best friend' (mostly these will be what can be described as 'strong ties')
- acquaintance – having a network of acquaintances
- membership – being a member of associations and organizations
- keeping in touch – with trends and movements of interest, subscribing to them, belonging to 'social worlds'
- being part of a family – having an active connection with family life
- having a partner: or someone to whom a long-term commitment has been made
- being a neighbour – living next door to, or at least near to, someone (down the street or across the road)
- knowing or being known in a neighbourhood – using the resources of the neighbourhood (usually the area within easy walking distance from where you live) and recognising and being recognised by others who use them too.[28]

In their book, *Members of Each Other*, John O'Brien and Connie Lyle O'Brien examine this issue in some depth. They cite evidence of friendships between people with disabilities and non-disabled people, attempt to define the components of friendship and examine some of the challenges it presents. One of the key challenges is the power imbalance, a result of differences in income, social networks and capability. In consequence:

- the person without power may experience their difference in power profoundly the other may take their power for granted
- when a person with a wide network and lots of connections, is friends with a person with narrow networks and limited connections, the imbalance may lead to confusion – both may be unclear as to what is expected or what each has the right to demand of the relationship
- people without power and control who have suffered from people leaving them may feel they need to 'test' a friend before they can trust them
- friends may worry they have not done enough for the person if they feel they have failed to deal with injustices or gain the cooperation of services.

Despite these potential difficulties the O'Brien's believe that:

> estimating a low potential for friendship because of apparent differences between people reflects a narrow and flat appreciation of friendship and how it grows.[29]

They conclude that friendships between people with and without disabilities are not only possible but also essential in creating a 'modest revolution' against the way our society discriminates against those with disabilities.

A group of people who have set out to create a 'modest revolution' are the members of the Speaking for Ourselves self-help and self-advocacy group in Philadelphia. They have formed a partnership scheme amongst members and advisors that enables people to support each other more effectively. Some of these partnerships have naturally evolved into friendships. One partner, Bea, summed up what she gains from her relationship with Karen:

> I enjoy having Karen as a partner. I mean I think it's been a real mutual enjoyment for both of us. I guess I've enjoyed having Karen for a friend as much as I've enjoyed any other woman as a friend . . . It makes my life fuller for me.[30]

Everyone engaged in this work needs to examine this issue for themselves. There is still a widespread assumption that it is impossible for disabled people to truly be friends with non-disabled people. Many of 'us' believe that 'they' are better off with their 'peer group'. It is an issue that challenges our deepest values and rests on how far we can accept the ability of disabled people to contribute to our society.

Another Speaking for Ourselves partner, Sharon, pinpoints this when describing her relationship with DeWeese:

> Perhaps I have been disappointed in the partnership now and again. But it's because of me: I'm a person who's so oriented to caring and fixing things and, you know, making things good for people, that I don't always see my own needs. And so I think that one way I'm disappointed . . . is that I'm just not vulnerable enough. And DeWeese is really teaching me that, just as he can tell me and talk to me about anything, he would like me to be able to do that too with him . . . And I think it's very important in a partnership to have that. I've also learned a lot about what I would call caring and not curing. When you're talking to someone, not trying to give advice or fix everything up but just to listen and be someone who's there . . .[31]

Some people in the disability movement feel that too much emphasis is placed on friendships developing between disabled and non-disabled people.

> Disabled people's desire to be accepted by non-disabled people has been a cause of internal discrimination. I believe that we must first accept ourselves and then if non-disabled people don't accept us, so be it.[32]

To some, the assumption that disabled people should be integrated into 'normal society' is oppressive. French, for one, argues that this assumption ignores the benefits derived from friendships between disabled people.[33]

In her research looking at the relationships of three people with disabilities Chris Jones found that:

> two of the disabled participants appeared to be experiencing more reciprocity in relationships with other disabled people ... Whilst the researcher acknowledges the potentially damaging consequences of grouping disabled people together solely on the basis of label, it is suggested that the status of the person as disabled or non-disabled appears to be less important than the choice of both parties to enter into the relationship and the mutual benefits gained.[34]

Normalisation and person centred planning have been widely interpreted as being against relationships between people with disabilities. However, in both these approaches, it is not a matter of whether disabled people choose friendships with other disabled people, but of whether they also have the opportunity to choose relationships with non-disabled people – so that they have choice. At present, many people have neither that experience nor that opportunity.

PRACTICE IN DEVELOPING FRIENDSHIPS

For many people with disabilities opportunities to develop relationships have been limited from a very early age. As a consequence, they have few precedents for forming relationships. In an article in *Community Living* Jenny Barrett recounts the experience of a member of staff:

> [he] happened to observe his service user meeting an acquaintance on the street. The service user did not respond to what the other person was saying and in effect the 'conversation' consisted of two people talking about two different things.[35]

We take for granted all the playground experiences we had as children that enabled us to understand interaction with others. People with disabilities have often missed out on these formative lessons. In both a conscious way and by example, staff can play an invaluable role in helping the people they work with learn more about friendships. Some people won't need this support, but for others listening, reciprocating invitations, giving and receiving affection will be unfamiliar practices and will bring up unfamiliar feelings. It is important that individuals have the chance to talk over new experiences and are given support in what may be a new role for them. Discussing this openly is essential. We can be concerned not to interfere in other people's relationships but when someone

has limited experience of developing relationships she may lose a potential friend if she doesn't have support and encouragement.

FRIENDSHIPS BETWEEN STAFF AND SERVICE USERS

Sometimes a individual can become confused about the difference between a paid staff member and a friend. Sometimes both the staff member and the focus person would define the relationship as a friendship. Training in the social-care field tends to emphasize the importance of maintaining boundaries between staff and individuals. This is often for very good reasons – to maintain objectivity, to avoid confusing staff needs with those of the focus person, and to prevent 'burn-out'. However staff experiences show that it is not always that clear. It is hard to legislate against emotional attachment. Sometimes staff may feel friendship towards someone they support. They may get on so well with them that they invite them to their homes to meet their families. They may feel that this is the quickest way to achieve inclusion for them.

Zana Lutfiyya has researched and written about the nature of friendships between staff and clients. She accepts as friendship a situation in which both the staff member and the client define themselves as friends. She concludes that:

> people with disabilities and paid caregivers can establish and enjoy genuine friendships with each other. As with all friendships, it is important to recognize and value these relationships.

But she cautions against:

- complications caused by the conflict of interest sustained by a friend who is also employed by the agency that supports the client
- exaggerating the extent of these friendships – *'the well-established and powerful role of "client" and "staff" form a rocky soil, making it difficult for friendships to take root and flower'*
- assuming that staff have to be friends with clients in order to provide a good service
- assuming that friendships with staff are all a client needs.[36]

Agencies react differently to friendships between individuals and staff. Some attempt to forbid such relationships, seeing them as unprofessional and a potential risk to both the staff member, who could be assaulted or harassed, and the individual, who becomes vulnerable to abuse.

One staff member working for such an agency feels restricted within this culture. She believes it is *'difficult to care for someone you don't care about'* and feels that such a policy doesn't allow for the personal judgement of staff members. She is keen to invite the people she likes to meet her family and wanted to invite one individual she supports home for Christmas. She did not do so because she knew that the agency would view it as unfair on other users of the service. Individuals supported by that agency, and staff that work there, miss out on valuable opportunities to develop relationships with each other.

Other, less traditional, agencies have gone to practically the opposite extreme by developing a culture in which the invitation of focus people into the lives of staff members is almost compulsory. One staff member working for just such an agency felt that this led to burn-out and resentment because staff did not feel that they had a choice about who to befriend.

The overriding lesson seems to be one of letting staff members and the people they support decide for themselves. However, we should always remember that:

- there will always be a power imbalance between someone paid to support and the focus person
- the duty of care may mean that occasionally staff need to act in ways they would not do with other friends
- friendship with service users may bring staff members into conflict with employers
- making friends with a service user has an effect on other service users and on other staff members in a team
- it may be the only friendship in the service user's life and may therefore carry unusual significance.

These issues need to be faced honestly and discussed openly with the service user and, if necessary, the team.

SEXUAL FRIENDSHIPS

Sadly, in our work researching this book we came across very little evidence of attempts by agencies to encourage and support the sexual relationships of people with disabilities. However, as one parent put it:

> It is easy for many people to espouse the belief that every person, even one with the most severe disabilities, has a right to be a social, sexual person; however, it is quite another matter to take an active role in proposing specific goals that will secure that right.

She goes on to propose five responsibilities of providers:

1. To develop a broad philosophy and resulting policies and procedures that support and affirm the sexual rights and responsibilities of people with disabilities.
2. To hire staff willing to support and act on these policies and procedures and managers trained and experienced in sexuality training, education and counselling.
3. To provide ongoing training on sexuality to all staff (taking staff turnover into account).
4. To set clear guidelines and procedures to protect against sexual abuse.
5. To actively promote positive attitudes and approaches toward sexuality within the agency's programmes, among parents and families, in the local community, and in the professions represented in the agency – e.g. to disavow terms such as perversion and sexual inadequacy, and to confront the lack of understanding that is distortive and demeaning to people with disabilities.[37]

In this book we take the view that providing opportunities for connecting in communities paves the way for deeper relationships. Support agencies need to be aware of this and must be prepared to support it to address the challenges it may generate.

Often services are designed and delivered in a way that is more convenient for the service rather than the focus person. Yet, inflexible service provision will not help individuals to develop the full range of relationships that those who do not live in 'service-land' have the freedom to enjoy.

In service planning, and frequently even in so-called person centred planning, there is often such an emphasis on planning to go out, go to college or to get a job, that planners sometimes miss the fact that what people actually want most is to spend time with the person they love, homemaking and being together in a relationship.

WHAT HAVE WE LEARNT ABOUT THE NATURE OF FRIENDSHIP AND DISABILITY SO FAR?

So far in the debate, the argument seems to be that it is presumptuous to judge the nature and quality of the relationships of others. In her study of four

friendships involving people with and without disabilities, Zana Lutfiyya discovered that the meaning of any friendship is created by the ways in which its participants enact and talk about it:

> Commonalty, equality, mutuality and comprehension are best understood from the perspective of the friends themselves, rather than according to the measurements of the detached observer.[38]

In our work we have experienced the importance of reciprocity between people, particularly when friendships develop between staff and those who use services. Robert Perske sums this up:

> Both people must profit from a friendship. The nature of the personal invigoration and enrichment may, of course, differ for each person. Yet, each person must leave a friendship with something. Otherwise, all efforts in the relationship will lead to an agonizing and boring trip down a poorly paved, one-way street called 'benevolence' a street that will ultimately intersect with another called 'obligation'.

At the same time, we need to question some of our everyday assumptions about friendship. Is it always necessary for us to have relationships in which we give and receive equally all the time? Do we all not give more in some relationships and receive more in others? If we see all our relationships as contributing to a more general social capital then we can happily give more at one time to one particular individual, while trusting that we will get it back at another from somebody else.

In this work the O'Briens warn us:

> . . . to be careful never to compromise the human dignity of people with . . . disabilities and cautious not to betray hope with inflated stories of easy success or perfect relationships.[39]

In this chapter, we have attempted to clarify the community connecting task by offering definitions of the key words 'community' and 'friendship'. In the next chapter, we begin to think about getting to know the person through:

- person centred planning
- 'being with' the person in their life
- creating a portfolio.

chapter two
discovering the 'real' person

Why am I afraid to tell you who I am? If I tell you who I am, you may not like who I am, and that is all that I have.

John Powell

The foundation of relationships building is to learn about ourselves and each other, our gifts, interests and relationships.

Person centred planning offers different 'windows' that can be used to highlight areas of a person's life, as they share stories and describe dreams. If an individual already has a person centred plan, (for example a Personal Futures Plan or an essential lifestyle plan),[40] then this will provide a head start for them if they want to think about connecting in their community. They will already have done some work identifying their gifts, skills, interests and dreams.

However, it's not necessary to be familiar with all the tools of person centred planning in order to embark on connecting in community. Sometimes just a glimpse of an individual's dreams or existing relationships will lead to further opportunities; in other cases more detailed work will be necessary. In this chapter, we demonstrate how some of the different 'windows' from person centred planning can be a useful starting point for the task of helping someone to build community.

The collection of information that emerges through the process of gathering information forms a 'portfolio'. This can be used again and again for reflection and direction as the work on community connecting takes shape.

As the John Powell quote indicates, getting to know someone involves trust and needs to be undertaken sensitively.

This chapter covers:

- person centred planning
- creating a portfolio
- windows to look at someone's life
- exploring what the person wants from their connections

In the next chapter we explain how this information can be used in beginning the search for community connections.

PERSON CENTRED PLANNING

Person centred planning is a process of continual listening and learning, focused on what is important to individuals now and in the future, and acting upon this in alliance with their family and friends. It is the collective term for a variety of techniques used to get to know a person, develop an understanding of that person's hopes for the present and the future, and to set priorities for change.

> Getting to know the person gives us a chance to break through stereotypes, professional roles, and impersonal approaches to find a new way to see people and feel the person work for change.[41]

Helping people to achieve the lifestyle they desire now and the hopes they have for the future requires learning who they are as people and what is important in their lives. A useful place to start developing a better understanding of individuals is to find out about the people they associate with, the places they go, and the activities they do. This involves being with them in different situations and settings and listening very carefully to them – to their behaviour as well as their words. John O'Brien describes this as 'listening with your heart'.[42] If individuals do not use words to communicate, discovering the ways in which they do express themselves would be the first step.

This is not an 'assessment'.[43] It is a shared journey of learning to discover what Beth Mount calls the 'rich folklore of people'. This means gathering as much information as possible, noticing themes and discerning what is important. It need not take a great deal of time, but this will depend on how much the individual can participate and on how many other people who know the person well are involved.

There are three main ways to really learn about someone:

- listening to them
- spending time with them in different situations and settings
- talking with others who know them well.

Listening to the person

As we have said, really listening to someone means listening to their words and to the things they say through their actions and behaviour. People reveal important things about themselves in all sorts of situations. Not much is learnt by sitting down with someone for a formal interview with specific questions. Instead we need to have conversations that allow people to tell and show what is important to them and be constantly vigilant and alert to pick up on what the individual is communicating in other ways. Rather than gather all the information in one conversation, it may be more helpful to harvest opportunities as they emerge throughout the day – for example, talking about favourite and least favourite breakfasts over breakfast in the morning.

People who work in one-to-one support roles with individuals will already have developed their skills in this area, but here they will be using them in a very specific context. When having these sorts of conversations with someone, especially where a person has limited life experiences, it is important not to ask leading questions. It is equally important not to limit what someone wants to say because of preconceptions of what is possible or not. In addition, it is crucial that people are supported to record their own information in a way that makes sense to them, whether using words or pictures, photographs or video.[44]

Whatever method is used to gather and record information, the first task should always be to find out good things about people. Asking, first of all, what individuals like about themselves, and then asking others what they like and admire about them. This will offer a very strong foundation for the work of community connecting.

Stan's story

Stan and Karen worked together for three months to help Stan think about what was important in his life and what he wanted to change. Stan is twenty-eight and lives in North Manchester with another man called Pete, supported by staff. Every week Karen and Stan spent about an hour together talking, taking photos, and describing memories. Together they started to make up a portfolio.

When Karen first met Stan, one of his staff had told her that Stan had a photo of his sister's wedding but not much else. It was actually Stan's foster brother's wedding, and Stan brought out three albums of photographs, which were his most precious possessions and which his worker had not been aware of.

Stan had not had any photos taken of himself in the last seven years and had very few of the time between leaving his foster parents, at the age of thirteen, and his twenty-first birthday, which he had spent in the long-stay hospital. Stan showed Karen some photos that no one else in the house knew about because he had decided that they were too important to show staff in case they got damaged. He decided he wanted to put copies of two of them into the portfolio.

Stan also wanted to have some photos of himself now, doing things that he enjoyed. Later he described this as one of the things he thought was important about the process. When they had finished, they had clear ideas about what Stan wanted to change and wanted to talk about with other people and also about things that he did not want to mention. Stan had had alcohol problems in the past. Unlike most people who can 'lose' their past by moving jobs or moving areas if they want to, Stan's past misdemeanours were brought up at every planning meeting and he wanted that to stop.

Through the process of thinking about what was important to him, and having time to do this at his own pace, Stan told Karen that he hated his job and they talked about ways that he could change it.

Stan and Karen used the portfolio to prepare for Stan's planning meeting. Together they transferred the information that Stan wanted to share at his meeting onto posters. Stan chose who he wanted to come and arranged to have the meeting at his house. At the meeting he enjoyed selecting people to read each section and then he talked about it and told people what he wanted to be different. Together they agreed on what they could all do to change things.

At Stan's previous planning meetings, the goals had been 'to have more independence' and 'to be self medicating', but now people were planning to help Stan pursue his new found interest in taking photos, to change jobs, and to look for opportunities to meet someone with whom he could have a lasting relationship.

The staff commented on how much they had learned about Stan. Even though some of them had worked with Stan for over three years, they discovered things about him that they had not been aware of before.

Spending time with the person

To learn what life is like for someone, it sometimes helps to 'walk with the person in her shoes'. This might be all the more essential if that person does not use words to communicate. It is important to spend time with the person in all sorts of different situations, doing a range of different activities with a variety of people, and at different times of the day and week.

These may include:

- sharing a meal
- going to a leisure activity together
- spending some of a weekend, a weekday morning or an afternoon together
- spending an evening together
- being there when there is not much going on
- attending a meeting with the person
- trying an activity that is new to the person.

Listening to others who know the person

Other people can add valuable information about what seems important to the focus person, what makes her tick, what makes her happy or sad or angry, as well as what her past has been like. It can be immensely helpful to share insights and ideas about what works and doesn't work for someone. Enlisting help from other people at this stage can be a foundation for encouraging people to become involved later in developing opportunities and making connections.

By listening and learning from other people, rich, colourful details can be added to the picture of who the individual is. A relationship circle is a helpful way to illustrate who is part of the person's life, and therefore who can be enlisted to share the journey. Later in this chapter we describe what a relationship circle is and how to complete one. Each person you talk to from the relationship circle could have important contributions to make.

One way to start is to ask each person what they like and admire about the focus person and when they last had a good time together, as a way of discovering what the relationship is like. The questions about 'like' and 'admire' and 'fun' will reveal whether the person has a close personal relationship with the individual. If the person does not have a close relationship with the individual then they will be unlikely to have information that will be helpful in this context, although they may have crucial information that relates to how to keep the person healthy and safe. The kind of people who are the most useful are those who spend a significant amount of time with the focus person, who have a close relationship with them now or have had in the past and who have lots of positive things to say about them. However, it is important not to overlook or dismiss people just because they don't spend very much time with the individual; some people get very close after only a very short time together.

> If people with disabilities are to achieve the lifestyle they desire, we need to understand them. Understanding requires insight, empathy and time. The time that it takes to understand the person can be shortened by using the accumulated knowledge of people who know and care about the individual.[45]

CREATING A PORTFOLIO

> When supporting someone else to create a personal portfolio we start from the premise that we all have gifts. This means that we all have a wealth of talent, skills, knowledge and unique personal qualities. In some of us, these gifts may be as yet untapped, unrecognised, hidden or ignored. It is the job of the facilitator to find clues to uncover these gifts.[46]

Once information has been gathered, there are lots of different ways to record it or to make it into a 'portfolio'. The individual might find it useful to have all the information summarised on large pieces of paper, for example. Sometimes people invite their friends and family to do this work together at a meeting. Other people might prefer to have a series of regular sessions to gather the information, as Stan did with Karen in the earlier story.

We all record our own lives in different ways, for example:

- a memento box of objects that reflect important events, people or times in your life
- a photo album that documents your life from birth to present day
- researching and drawing your family tree
- scrap books of special times, such as holidays
- a video showing ordinary and special times in your life
- audio tapes of children learning to talk or other events
- a notice board or large clip frame with photos of important people or special times
- a diary.

The word 'portfolio' describes a collection of information about someone's life. Most people have employment or education portfolios, students complete portfolios of their work, and in employment many people have personal-development plans that form part of their personal portfolio.

Person centred planning gathers a lot of different information about people, for example, their history, what they like to do, who they know, and where they go. This portfolio of information will reflect and illustrate the person's experiences and achievements, as well as her dreams and hopes for the future. When people are supported to record their own story it can give them more control over what they want to record and share, rather than having someone else describe their life. Individuals are encouraged to record and represent their information in a way that reflects their ideas and gifts. This could include photographs, audiotape, artwork, letters, certificates, videos, and objects – anything that expresses something about their life and who they are. The members of People First in Manchester have compiled descriptions of their lives using different media, called them personal portfolios and presented this way of working on a video. Multimedia profiles are another way of recording and sharing personal information.

Portfolios such as these provide an invaluable source of information about an individual that is particularly useful when there is turnover in that person's support.

Sally's story

Sally took a different approach to recording her life over a number of years. The different ways that she has collected information and memories about her life can be called a 'personal portfolio', but to Sally it is her life story.

Sally lives in a group home with four other people with high support needs. She is an attractive woman in her mid-twenties. Brought up in a small town in Scotland, Sally moved to the city four years ago. She comes from a very close, Catholic family.

When she moved to her new home, Sally began to record her story. She needed to tell all the new people she met about herself. With the help of a member of staff who she is close to she wrote down her 'life story' and illustrated it with photographs.

Sally communicates using a Bliss board. She tells how at birth she almost died. She had breathing difficulties and was diagnosed as having cerebral palsy. The doctors told her mother that she would be a vegetable and one of the nurses said that she would be better off dead. For the first twenty years of her life, Sally lived at home with her parents, her brother and her sister. She was well cared for and very well protected. She attended a special school near her home where she was assessed but was thought incapable of ever learning to read. Her childhood was a constant round of medical treatment and assessment. Sally says that because of her disability she was over-protected. Before she moved away from home, most of her time was spent either at special school, with her family, at church or receiving medical treatment. It wasn't until her mid-twenties that she began making decisions for herself and becoming more independent.

Her personal portfolio includes a book that has photos of her family with labels underneath saying who they are and how they are related to her. It also includes photos of her as a child, with her brother and sister and at her first Holy Communion. She tells stories about when she first went to school she pretended not to like some foods. Her teacher rumbled her when she came round to the house and found her happily tucking in to everything that was offered. These stories have been written down by Sally's support worker and pasted into the book.

Sally's experiences at the group home are charted on a large sheet of paper. The photos here are of her holidays in Oxford, York and at Lourdes. There are illustrations describing how she is looking for her own flat, how she now travels to the day centre in a taxi rather than by special bus, and how she attends classes in Biology and Religious Education at a mainstream school. Sally has written statements beside the photos: 'I enjoy a good laugh'; 'I am now more confident about making decisions and expressing preferences'; 'I am more assertive'.

Sally still has numerous medical records that are kept at home as well. These records give us crucial information about her health, but Sally's own way of recording her story tells us about who she really is.

WINDOWS TO LOOK AT SOMEONE'S LIFE

These windows are taken from established person centred planning processes, particularly Personal Futures Planning[47] and essential lifestyle planning.[48] There are six windows that people can use to begin the journey of community connecting. They are:

1. Relationships
2. Gifts
3. Skills and Interests
4. Hopes and Dreams
5. How to Provide Good Support
6. How I Spend My Time

There are many others that you can use as needed. Some windows may seem more useful than others. Choose together and start with whichever one interests the focus person most.

It is important that anyone undertaking this kind of work with an individual should understand what it feels like. The best way to do this is to try it out for yourself first. Sharing personal information can be a very important first step in shifting the balance of power, as well as being a great way to explain the process. When sharing this kind of information, however, it is clearly necessary to be sensitive to some of the contrasts that exist between different people's lives, and to consider the impact of showing a very full relationship map to someone who only has three or four paid staff in their life.

1. Relationships

This window is useful:

- for finding out who could contribute to getting the person connected
- for identifying relationships that could be developed or strengthened
- for showing the balance of family, friends and paid workers in the person's life.

The deepening and expanding of relationships is fundamental to community connecting. The process begins by identifying with the focus person, existing relationships that are important.

Judith Snow developed a simple way of illustrating the different relationships in a person's life.

Relationships map

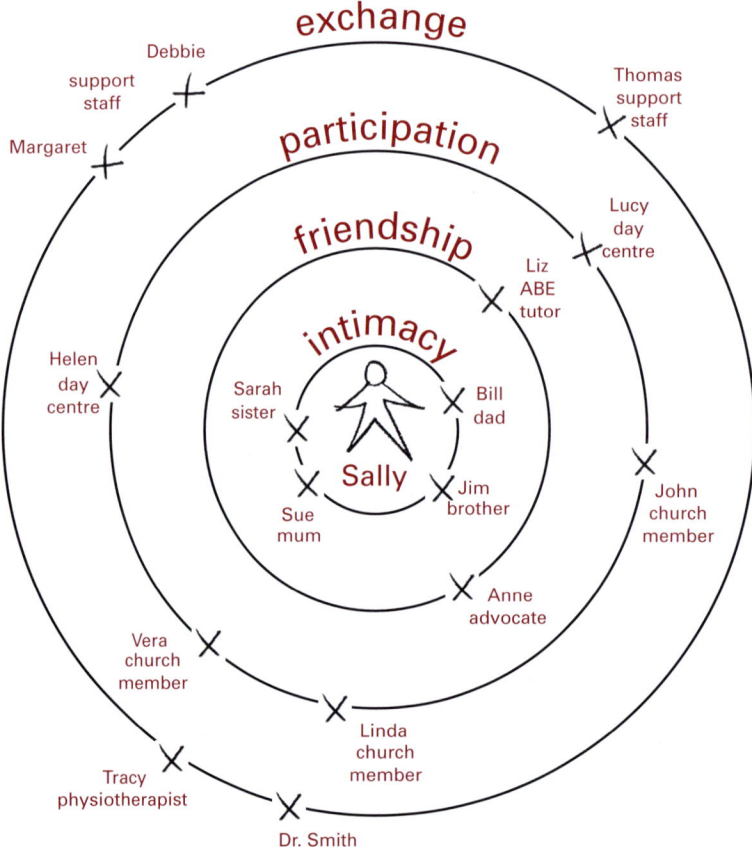

Exchange – people in this circle will be those who are paid to be in the person's life: e.g. paid carers, other service providers, shopkeepers and postman etc.

Participation – people who share experiences and interests with the person: e.g. work colleagues, members of the same club or church.

Friendship – people who simply choose to spend time with the person and share the enjoyment of each other's company.

Intimacy – those closest to the person: close family, partners and loved friends.

Completing the relationship circle

The focus person's name or photo should go in the middle of the inner circle. She might want to represent people in the other circles by writing their names, inserting photos, or drawing pictures or symbols. If people are included who are no longer involved in the person's life then it might be useful to note how long they have been absent. Sometimes the map can only be done as a 'best guess' on behalf of the person along with someone who knows the her well. It is important to remember that close relationships occur regardless of roles and responsibilities – people may have friendships with administrative, maintenance, and professional staff.

Questions to ask

- Who is most important in your life?
- Who else do you see often? (Family, neighbours, people at work or at the day centre, people you see in the evenings or weekends)
- Who do you celebrate special occasions with, e.g. Christmas or your birthday?
- Is there anyone you feel close to that you have not seen for a while?
- How often do you see each of the people you have mentioned?
- Do you see them by themselves or as part of a group?
- Who makes the arrangements to meet up?

Once the circles are complete, it will be possible to look together at any themes or patterns in the relationships. Are, for example, most of the people paid staff or other people with disabilities? How close is the person's family? Does the person have any contact with neighbours or local people?

2. Gifts

This window is essential:

- for showing what the person enjoys, is good at, and can contribute to
- for identifying things that the person may want to do more often
- for starting to think about the kinds of people the person gets on well with.

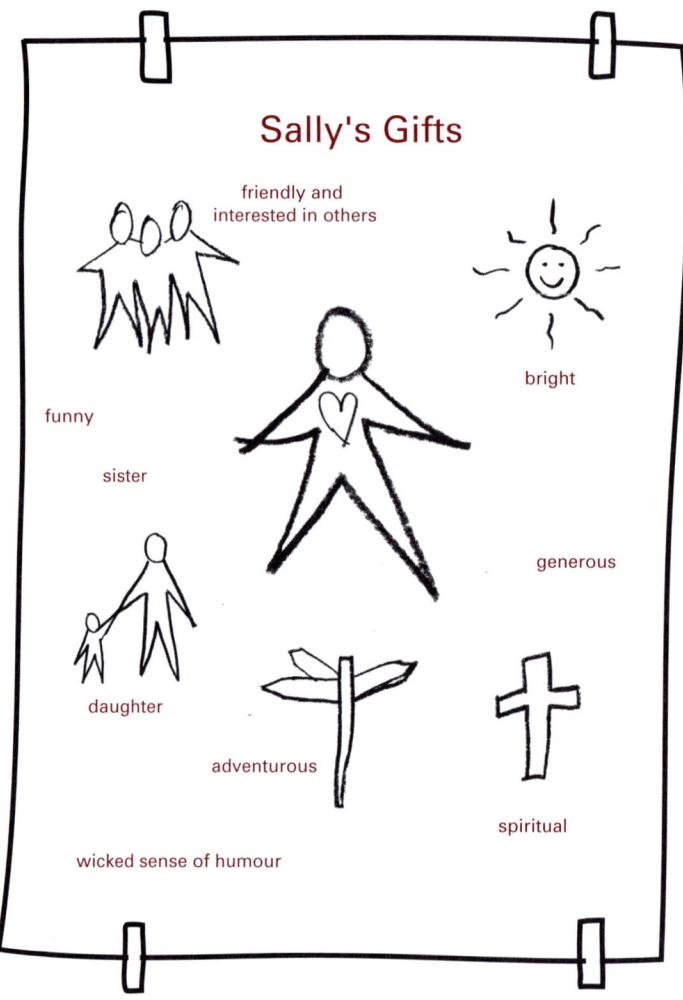

Our gifts are what make us attractive to the other people we meet. Beyond being simply our interests or abilities they are the parts of us that other people warm to – the parts of us that make people want to spend time with us: our personal Velcro.

Gifts can be anything from a warm smile or cheeky sense of humour, to a concern for others, courage, or honesty.

> Identifying, developing and expanding personal qualities and gifts is another key to opening windows to community life. By naming and claiming the positive aspects of a person's identity, we help strengthen a growing sense of self that can be developed in community life.[49]

To be successful in making our communities more inclusive we need to believe that every individual has gifts to offer other people, indeed that the community as a whole will benefit from including everyone. In that way we need, like Millie O'Connell, to be unashamed idealists:

> The community . . . loses something when it exiles people into the social service system. It loses the gift of each individual: those who are exiled, like the rest of us, have their own beauty and their own potential ... When the community cuts itself off from people who are disabled, it also denies part of what it is to be human. A community that has no place for those who cannot speak, or walk, or do higher mathematics is finally impoverishing itself.[50]

This attitude is not always an easy one to adopt. In Britain we tend, as a people, to focus on what we lack rather than on what we have, what we can't do rather than what we can. Even so, we are unlikely to introduce ourselves to strangers with the words 'I'm divorced, I'm under-achieving at work and I crashed into my neighbour's car last night.' We should not then routinely describe people with support needs as 'loners', 'mentally handicapped' and 'clumsy'.

Most of us have been brought up to believe that people with disabilities are not like us. We have been schooled to look at what is wrong with them rather than what is right. Like the rest of society we have grown up feeling sorry for disabled people – for their lack of ability – and find it hard to see the individual before seeing a medical condition.

Some of the people we support undoubtedly make it hard for us to see their gifts sometimes, but many with disabilities have been let down all their lives and may find it difficult to trust and open themselves to new people as a result. They may think themselves unlovable and adopt behaviour that asks others to verify that. Getting to know people, and being trusted enough to see their gifts takes time.

> As one direct staff person expressed, 'I can't ask somebody else to do what I'm not willing to'. The staff or persons who are acting as community connectors must care deeply about, fully appreciate, and be willing to spend time themselves with the individual whom

they are supporting to be in relationships. If the connector is not willing to have a personal relationship with the person, it is unlikely that he or she will be successful in asking a community member to be in a relationship with that individual. The key factor here is not that the connectors must develop their own friendship with each individual with disabilities, but rather that they would have the types of feelings, caring and liking that they would be willing to do so.[51]

This distinction is important. Although we do not have to be friends with everyone we support, we do have to appreciate the qualities in them that would enable others to be friends with them. Inevitably, there may be some people we support who we don't like, whose gifts we will never be able to see. If we cannot see an individual's gifts then we will never be able to communicate them to anyone else and will be unable to help that person make connections with other people.

If nobody in the person's life can see her gifts then that person is in trouble. Immediate steps need to be taken to plan with the individual, with the aim of finding out why no one can see the good in her. Immediate action needs to be taken to change her situation.

People with disabilities are often considered solely in terms of their deficiencies, but this only contributes to predictions of a bleak future. In person centred planning, 'giftedness' is used to mean 'unique attributes' rather than 'talents'. Used in this sense, a person's gifts provide a key to unlocking connections within the community.

> . . . all people are gifted. This thought sounds strange to us because we are used to understanding gifts to be special talents that only a few individuals possess . . . if a person can play classical piano at age four or run twenty-six miles in one day without breathing very hard at the end of it or add a long column of five digit numbers without a calculator – if someone has such talents as these they are gifted . . . everyone has gifts – countless ordinary and extraordinary gifts. A gift is anything that one is or has or does that creates an opportunity for a meaningful interaction with a least one other person. Gifts are the fundamental characteristics of our human life and community . . . There are two simple gifts that all people have and that every other gift depends on. The first is presence. Since you are here you are embodying the possibility of meaningful interaction with someone else . . . Secondly you are different from everyone else – in countless ways. Difference is required to make meaning possible . . . human interaction arises from presence and difference. You are different from the next person in hundreds, perhaps thousands of ways – in your body, your thinking, your experience, your culture, your interests, tastes and desires, your possessions, your relationships, and more. Therefore you are a bundle of hundreds, perhaps thousands of gifts. So is everyone else.[52]

We often need other people to help us to think about what our gifts might be. Here are some questions that Michael Smull uses to ask others about gifts and contributions:

- What do others like and admire about Nazeem?
- Why do people choose to spend time with Nazeem?
- What have the people who like and admire Nazeem learned from her?
- How has Nazeem made a difference in their lives? What has she contributed?
- Where else may these contributions be appreciated in the community?

'People became more powerful when they were reminded of their gifts and they had a vision of how to change their lives.'[53]

3. Skills and Interests

This window is useful:

- for showing what the person enjoys or has a passion for
- for showing what talents the person has and the things they are good at
- for showing what the person can contribute
- for identifying things that the person may want to do more often
- for identifying the places, people and activities that make the person happy.

There is an obvious crossover between this window and the 'Gifts' window. An interest or a passion for something is also a gift because it creates the possibility for a connection with other people. It is important to differentiate between the two, so that the less tangible gifts do not get ignored, but it is not necessary to spend lots of time trying to decide precisely what is an interest and what is a gift. The most important thing is that everything is recorded.

Many people have existing hobbies and interests, some of which may be hidden to the casual observer.

> When I first started to support Zoe I had no idea what a fan she was of Monopoly. It was only when I asked her specific questions about her interests that she cautiously revealed to me that she had a special edition 'Gold' Monopoly set that she kept hidden away from staff because it was enormously valuable to her.

Other people have passions that are overlooked simply because the people who generally spend time with them do not value them.

> John has always had a passion for trains. He loves to spend time at the local train station watching the trains come and go and recording their numbers in a book. He will spend hours in his room logging his information and will then spend hours trying to tell anyone who will listen about the trains he has seen that day. The staff in John's house thought that he should work to control his obsession and try to relate more to other people in the house about other things. He was considered to have obsessive tendencies and it was felt that they should not be encouraged. However, when a member of staff really thought about John's gifts and how he could make connections with other people, the most obvious place to start was with his passion for trains. Looking for opportunities for John to spend time with other trainspotters was a very good place to begin to help John to make connections.

Questions to ask about interests

- What hobbies or activities make you excited and enthusiastic?
- In what ways do you like to help other people?
- Do you have interests that you used to pursue and would like to try again?
- What makes a good day for you?

Describing a good day from morning to evening might reveal interests or hobbies that have never been formalised or even identified.

For example, if I describe what makes a good day for me from the time I get up in the morning, one essential component is that I get to sing very loudly to chart music in the car on the way to work. This probably would never come up if you asked me what my hobbies are, but it is a very important part of who I am and helps me start the day in a positive frame of mind. If I was thinking about making connections for myself, I might start by trying to build on my love of singing in the car or my love of chart music.

4. Hopes and Dreams

This window is useful:

- for finding the direction that the person wants her life to go in
- for inspiring
- for bringing people together around a common purpose
- for getting a sense of what makes the person tick – what motivates her.

People dream in different ways. For people who are deprived and oppressed, the dream may be very small and simple – to have some peace and quiet, to be able to come and go.

Some people access their dream by thinking about what they would do if they won the Lottery or if they were told they only had six months to live. Their dreams might be about travelling or visiting people, studying, changing career or living in a particular place. Some people's dreams are more about a state of mind or about their spirit.

For other people their 'dream' is to have what is important to them in day-to-day life and focusing on what is important to them now may, therefore, be more significant than trying to identify dreams for the future. Sometimes you have to get a life before you can find your dream. This is particularly true for people who are ill or in crisis.

Often people use symbols when they dream. Sally dreamed about becoming a doctor. For her this symbolised being respected and knowing more about the way the body works. Another man we planned with talked about becoming Superman. His staff team thought this dream was drug related. In fact, when we explored it with him, he simply wanted to help people.

Dreaming can be emotional both for the individual and for those supporting them. Sometimes it is hard to face up to what we haven't done and maybe never can do.

> I guess one of the hardest times for me has been when Karen was very open to me about some of her dreams and my knowing there's nothing I can do to change things or help her. That's been very hard for me. Because there are times I would want to suggest to her to do something – something I would say normally to anybody – and yet I know that there are barriers for Karen. And I would like to just take those barriers and break them down so that I could see her dreams come true, the way she'd like to have them. That's been a very hard thing for me.[54]

Although Bea found listening to Karen's dream difficult, listening to someone's dreams is often a great inspiration to those who support an individual and can help them share in the desire to make those dreams come true.

Here are some questions to help people think about their hopes and dreams:

- In an ideal world, what would life look like for you? What would you be doing? Who is there? What does it sound, look, smell, and feel like?
- Take a moment and think about what gives direction to your life? What pulls you? What calls out to you? Describe the images, colours, smells, sounds, and feelings that give direction to your life.
- What kinds of relationships do you want in your life?
- Where do you dream of living?
- Are there adventures or experiences that you seek? Places that you would like to visit? New things that you have never tried?

When you are stuck

Some people may need help to develop their ideas about what they want. One way is to get people together in a small discussion group, using pictures, magazines and photos. Skills for People, a self-advocacy group based in Newcastle runs a course for self-advocates called 'Reach for the Stars' which does this.

Some person centred planning work was recently undertaken in a residential home for older people in Edinburgh. Initially, when the residents were asked to identify dreams for the future, they found it difficult to get started. Living in a group setting seemed to make some people reluctant to identify individual dreams, whilst others clearly felt that it would be impossible to achieve any dreams because of the limits of living in residential care. However, the facilitators kept trying and introduced the idea of the 'Wishing Tree'. They borrowed a model of a tree from the local school and made cardboard leaves to hang off the branches. The residents were encouraged to write their dreams on the leaves and then hang them on the tree. Having this visual aid not only made it easier for people to think of things but also made it more fun. A lot of dreams were identified, some large and some small, that people could then plan to act upon.

Exposure to new options and possibilities can also encourage people to desire a better situation. Conferences, meetings, discussions, and trips to other communities to learn about new options can have a significant impact on the development of a personal dream.

'When people desire something different for themselves, it is almost always because they have heard of a better situation from someone else.'[55]

5. How to Provide Good Support

This is useful:

- for identifying exactly what good support means for the person
- for describing in detail what people who support the person must do
- for seeing what support someone may need to participate in community opportunities
- for discovering what motivates the person
- for examining ways in which the person might be supported to become more independent.

How to Provide Good Support for Sally ...

• Sally uses an electric wheelchair – this needs to be charged-up when the red light flashes – Sally will let you know.

• Sally is allergic to nuts therefore all food should be checked.

• Sally doesn't like people leaning over her from behind.

• Sally doesn't like being touched apart from by close friends and family.

This section describes in detail what support an individual wants or needs as well as what works for and motivates her. The 'how to provide good support' window does not include things that the person can do for themselves.

This window should address any important health issues that need to be considered. Where there are issues of health that are sensitive and/or very personal, a judgement needs to be made about who needs to know the information and in what detail.

One way of recording this is to put items under two headings: 'what works' and 'what does not work' for the person. The 'what works' section may include how the person likes to be treated, what kinds of people she gets on with best, or what motivates her, for example praise and encouragement, rewards, small steps, celebrations, listening.

The 'what does not work' section may include the situations that frustrate or frighten her, when her energy levels are lowest, or when she gets bored or miserable.

To be successful in supporting a person means helping her to have more of what works for her and less of what doesn't.

Very often a key part of supporting someone to make connections in the community lies in understanding the way that that person communicates. A communication chart can be drawn up to enable new people to understand the individual better (for more on this see Appendix).

6. How I Spend My Time

This window is useful:

- for identifying the activities that the person is already involved in that may be a starting point for connections
- for understanding more about the person's preferences so that they can be expanded upon.

This window records the places that the individual goes during the day, week and year. Over a time span of this length it manages to cover both regular and occasional activities. It also lists of all the activities and places a person is involved in. It might also be helpful to record to what extent the person participates in the activities and who else is involved.

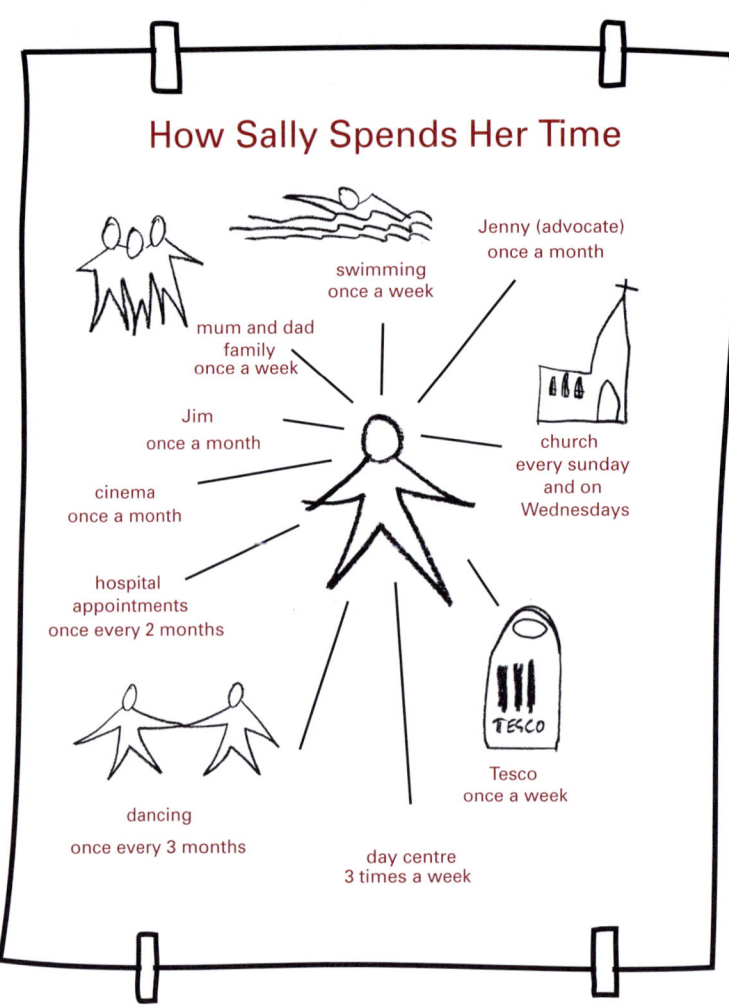

Questions to ask

- Where do you go during the week?
- Where do you go in the evenings and at weekends?
- Who do you go with? (Alone? With staff? With other people you live with?)
- Who makes the arrangements for the activity (e.g. who books the bowling alley, looks out bus times etc.)?
- Do you meet and get to know other people at these places or activities?
- Which of the activities do you enjoy the most?

Other Windows

There are many other areas of a person's life that could be useful to reflect on when making community connections. These include focusing on someone's history, nightmares or communication. Further information on these issues is provided in the Appendix.

LOOKING FOR PATTERNS AND THEMES

Once enough information has been gathered for the various 'windows' chosen, it might be useful to spend some time reflecting on what has been collated. It might be possible to identify patterns or themes, which could help point to a way forward.

Questions to ask

- What are the gifts and interests to appreciate and build on?
- What support and routines do we need to consider?
- What environments and places work best for her?
- Are there times of the day that work best for her?
- What is the person already doing that she would like to do more of?
- What would take her closer to her hopes and dreams?
- How much time does she spend in segregated activities?
- How much time does she spend doing things in groups and how much time alone or with one other person?
- Could any of the activities be adapted to create opportunities for meeting and getting to know other people?

WHAT DOES THE INDIVIDUAL WANT FROM THE CONNECTION?

Spending some time getting to know the person and using the windows will help work out what is missing in her life and what she might want from the connection. Robert Putnam uses the Yiddish distinction between 'machers' (the people who make things happen in a community) and 'schmoozers' (the people who have an active but less organized and purposeful social life). Every individual will have her own idea of what she would like her role in the community to be. Some want to do something particular in their community, whilst others would prefer just to have people to 'hang out' with.

What the individual ultimately wants out of the connection might not make a difference to where the work starts (after all, close friends normally develop from acquaintances), but it should make a difference to the end result. This needs to be identified from the beginning.

It will also make a difference to what is defined as success. The individual may not get a 'best friend' out of the connection but may have one more person in the street to say hello to – a person who could potentially introduce her to their network. It is important in this work to recognise that relationships work on many different levels and that there are different types of relationship, ranging from a lifelong friend to a passing acquaintance, which all have validity and value.

'Rather than grand successes, perhaps community building is made up of many small moments of connection.'[56]

This chapter has described how person centred planning represents a way of learning about each other through listening to the person, spending time together, and listening to others who know the person well. Different 'windows' from Personal Futures Planning and essential lifestyle planning have been offered as ways to get started in learning together with the individual. Information from these 'windows' can be creatively presented as a portfolio for the person providing clues that help begin the process of building relationships and connecting in communities.

chapter three
getting started

When we're trying to help people with disabilities meet new people, it helps to identify our own strategies, what's worked for us in the past. We can ask ourselves what we did, or how would we do it if we had to figure it out ourselves. The simplest question is, 'If this were me, what would I do?'

Angela Amado

In the previous chapter we concentrated on getting to know the person who wants to make connections, focusing on their gifts and what is missing from their lives. Now, we can start looking for opportunities to make connections.

Once the person's gifts have been identified, the next step is to think about how these gifts can be used so that they can ultimately lead to connections with other people and opportunities to make a contribution. There may be a very obvious starting point, for example, if the person has expressed a dream or preference, or if an idea has come from the individual's network or team. If not, there are several strategies that can be used to generate ideas. For instance:

- mapping the community for options (see Chapter Four)
- doing a network map and exploring options (see Chapter Five)
- doing our own network map (see Chapter Five)
- brainstorming ideas with colleagues (see the end of this chapter).

We will return to these strategies in the chapters that follow but before undertaking any of them there are some other fundamental considerations.

1. What is the role of the community connector and what is the agreement that is made with the person?
2. What is the best way of communicating the person's gifts to others? How should introductions be made?
3. What might get in the way of the person being able to communicate their gifts? What support might be put in place to get around these obstacles?
4. What are the risks involved for the person and what can be done to minimize these risks?

In this chapter we consider these four crucial issues in more depth. We finish by considering a number of ways of getting started.

1. WHAT IS THE ROLE OF THE COMMUNITY CONNECTOR AND WHAT IS THE AGREEMENT THAT IS MADE WITH THE PERSON?

Clarity from the outset will avoid confusion and dissatisfaction later on. It is essential that the person in the role of community connector and the focus person are both clear about:

*   What the focus person hopes to get out of the community connecting work. Being as specific as possible about the objectives will help both initially and at the stage of exit and evaluation of the work. 'What will we count as success?' is a useful question to ask to get some clear and explicit goals.
*   What role the community connector is playing – are they going to have a relationship with the person beyond the duration of the community-connecting work, or is it just for this one piece of work?
*   How long the community connector will work with the person – is it time limited or is it task-related?

Although this may sound very bureaucratic, it will help everyone to be clear about what is happening. If the community connector is not a friend, family member or part of the team, they will have to explain who they are, what they and the focus person are doing, and include family and friends and other workers. If they are already part of the support network, it would still be a good idea to be clear about this new aspect of their role.

Sometimes it helps to work up an agreement or contract between the community connector and the focus person, covering the points mentioned above.

2. WHAT IS THE BEST WAY OF COMMUNICATING THE PERSON'S GIFTS TO OTHERS? HOW SHOULD INTRODUCTIONS BE MADE?

The way that someone is introduced into a new situation or to a stranger is absolutely crucial if successful connections are to be made. As everyone knows, first impressions last. This means that community connectors may need to think about how they will behave with the person they are supporting. People in the community often take their lead from the person supporting an individual with a disability. Respect is always important, but when supporting an individual to make connections in the community it is crucial.

In addition, the person seeking connections should be supported to think about how they would like to be introduced to others. This should be thought out in advance, otherwise in the heat of the moment an unhelpful message may be conveyed that might put someone off. For example, it is easy to use labels, jargon or 'service speak', but ordinary language will be much more appropriate. One useful guideline is to describe the person '*in human terms, rather than human service jargon*'.[57]

Introductions need to focus on gifts and include only the information the community person needs to know in order to be able to accept and understand the focus person.

Additionally, it is sometimes necessary to explain one part of the person's behaviour so that other people are not immediately put off by it. Later we describe how while it can be possible to find a place where the behaviour of the focus person is completely acceptable, sometimes it works to simply explain it to other people so that they can understand what it means.

> When introducing an individual with a disability to a community member, there is a delicate balance to be struck. We need to provide enough information about the person so that the community members know what to expect or can respond to the individual's needs. We must also avoid giving information that's not really useful and might damage the individual's image and future relationships. The need to respect people's reputations is so crucial that it deserves careful attention.[58]

Choosing the right time is important. For instance, it may be best not to reveal everything in the initial phone call, but the community person may need to know of any likely behaviour before having to experience it directly. When explaining someone's behaviour, it is usually most honest and most respectful to specifically pinpoint the behaviour itself, rather than the label that often goes

with it – to put it in context and then explain how to deal with it. Sometimes, an explanation of where the behaviour has come from can be helpful but this should not be an opportunity for people to venture into psychoanalysis.

For example, the support worker could say to the community member: '*Julie sometimes snatches food. She spent a long time in hospital where people had to fight their corner. The best thing to do is to explain to her what she has done, take your own food back but offer her some more.*'

It may be necessary to tell the community person not to act in certain ways or do certain things.

For example: '*John hates crowded spaces. We don't know why this is but if you take him anywhere where there are lots of people in a small space he might start screaming. If this happens, you need to take him out, calmly, but as soon as possible.*'

It may also be necessary to explain how the focus person communicates.

For example: '*Sally doesn't use words to speak. Eyes up means no and eyes down means yes. She also uses a board with symbols on it, which she can point to.*'

As much as possible introductions and explanations should be devised with the focus person themselves so that she is comfortable with what is being said. Sometimes, if it is unclear whether the focus person understands, then her family or someone close to her might need to be involved as well.

Occasionally, the focus person might disagree about what information it is necessary to share with the community member. In situations such as this, we must tread very carefully, seek guidance from colleagues, and work until a satisfactory compromise is met. It would be a breach of confidentiality to reveal information about the focus person to a community member without their consent. So, it might be useful to go back and think again about the questions:

- Is it really necessary for the information about the individual to be known?
- Why does the individual not want the information to be shared?
- Is it an issue with the community person? Would she mind another member of the community knowing?
- Is it possible to change the behaviour or put in extra support so that the situation can be avoided?

- Could the information be conveyed in a way that would feel OK to the focus person?
- Would the individual feel more comfortable if the information was disclosed over time once she knows the community member better?

How introductions are made is probably one of the most critical factors affecting the success of community-building work. Many times, efforts at community connecting have been what human service agencies call 'educating the community' and have consisted of speeches or talks to churches or other groups on what people with disabilities are like and why group members should 'get involved'. Or, efforts to build community connections have consisted of a staff person saying to a community member, ' I work at the Village Group Home and the people there really need friends. Would you be interested in becoming somebody's friend?' Although both of these types of efforts have, from time to time, miraculously unearthed someone willing to become involved in an individual's life, they are far less productive than a more personal, one-to-one approach.[59]

For any strategy for connecting people to be successful, we need to think carefully about the best way to introduce them and how to support them by:

- introducing the person in a way that is both realistic and that emphasises her best qualities
- getting a balance between providing enough information for the community person to know what to expect or be able to respond to the individual's needs, and not giving information that is unnecessary or might damage the focus person's image and future relationships
- interpreting the communications of someone who does not use speech
- successfully managing out-of-the-ordinary behaviour
- making sure that the person is getting what they need in terms of support
- helping the future independence of the relationship by providing back-up support to the relationship without taking over
- giving individuals the chance to do what they can, and find ways to help the focus person make a genuine contribution.

One final point to remember is that, left to their own devices, people will very often successfully introduce themselves and, furthermore, will take great pleasure in introducing various people to each other. Any effort at community connecting needs to be about providing unobtrusive support and not about taking all the responsibility away from individuals themselves.

Helen was supporting a man who she had been told wanted to get to know his community better. He was someone with a very loud voice and speech that was not

very clear, so often people in the street recoiled from him because they didn't understand him. They spent time walking through his community, dropping into the local shops, having lunch in the cafes and often whiling away a few minutes sitting on a bench with a can of juice. It didn't take long to discover that he already had a huge number of connections and contacts in his community and one of the most powerful things for Helen was when he started to introduce her to people. What he needed help and support with was how to develop and deepen some of these passing acquaintances, but he certainly didn't need help introducing himself!

The introduction that is worked up by the individual and their support worker or community connector can form a part of their working agreement or contract (see below).

3. WHAT MIGHT GET IN THE WAY?

For man has closed himself up till he sees all things through the chinks in his cabin.

William Blake

Our key finding from getting to know people is a clear perception of their gifts – what they can offer other people and their community. Once we have a clear perception of this, and an idea of how to use it, we need to support individuals to communicate that side of themselves to others.

There are several reasons why this is more difficult for people with disabilities than for others

- as a society we are prejudiced against disability
- as individuals many of us have never met people with disabilities before and will see the disability before the person and be scared, dismissive or patronising
- people with disabilities have often had less practice at meeting others and making friends
- people with disabilities may have behaviour which is off-putting to others.

Mary O'Connell (1990) identifies some of the difficulties, rooted a lack of experience, that can limit some community association members' readiness to include people with disabilities:

66

- some people feel too busy to make time for a person who could require extra assistance – most active citizens balance work, family obligations, personal interests, and association duties and they may see including a person with a severe disability as a time consuming activity
- people with severe disabilities raise some people's doubts about their own competence to respond properly, the extent and limits of their responsibility, and their ability to deal with yet other's reactions to someone they assume is different – they don't see a disabled person as a potential contributor but as a kind of project
- some association leaders think of involving people with severe disabilities as a kind of extra activity that competes with the group's mission and perhaps exposes the association to new liabilities.

In our experience the main barrier between people with disabilities and people without disabilities is difference. We tend to see difference before we see sameness. The role of the community connector is to enable members of the community to see beyond the differences and focus on what is held in common. It is after this that people can begin to appreciate the differences.

Although changing the attitudes of society towards people with disabilities may seem a task beyond the remit of a community connector, every positive contact between a disabled person and someone who has never encountered disability before works towards it. However we may need to use more direct intervention as well. Tom Kohler talks about how part of the job of the community connector is to support the community member with whom we are trying to make the connection. We may need to allay their fears, challenge their prejudices or help them to communicate with the focus person. Mark Burton and Carolyn Kagan[60] suggest that as much time should be given to developing the competence of the community as to the social skills of disabled individuals. Many people will help when asked to. David Schwartz describes one American state's successful attempts to encourage communities to look after one another in his book *Crossing the River: Creating a Conceptual Revolution in Community and Disability.* But there are barriers.

Behaviour

Sometimes the people we support have behaviour that stands in the way of their meeting people. These need to be faced and planned for. There are several strategies that we can adopt.

The first and most obvious strategy for dealing with problem behaviour is to change it. The focus person can be supported to recognise the behaviour that prevents them connecting with other people, and to work on changing it. All of us can and do adapt our behaviour if given sufficient motivation. However, much of the time our behaviour is a sign of what we are feeling, and if those feelings change our behaviour changes too.

Dee left a long-stay hospital on the edge of town after a stay of over fifty years. During her stay at the hospital, Dee had gained notoriety as one of the 'problem people', someone who became violent and aggressive and who was persistently uncooperative. Like so many people who spend most of their life in the care of an institution, Dee left the hospital with an enormous quantity of notes and medical records which reinforced her dangerous and fearsome reputation.

Dee moved into a house in a quiet and genteel neighbourhood, which she was to share with four other ex-hospital residents, supported by a team of residential service workers.

However, although the five flat-mates were living in the community, they did not really participate in community life and they were not really included in their neighbourhood.

One of the factors which made it very difficult for Dee to be included as a valued and respected community member was the bad reputation that had followed her from her days in the hospital. As well as having a reputation for being violent and aggressive, Dee was also criticised for being inappropriately loud in public places:

'She's always wailing and moaning ... She's really loud, I can't take her anywhere', people would say about her.

It was true; Dee seemed never to be calm or quiet. She was forever making loud noises and always on the move. Because of this, many people found it difficult to be with Dee. It was difficult to share a space with her at home and even more difficult out in public.

Dee started working with a facilitator on a person centred plan and together they began to make a Relationship Map. In doing this, a window of opportunity opened up for Dee when the facilitator discovered that she had been very close to one of the nurses at the hospital, who had since retired. The facilitator contacted the ex-nurse and asked her to contribute to the person centred planning process. She was very willing to help and told lots of stories about good times they had shared together in the old hospital.

It came as a great revelation when the ex-nurse mentioned that they had regularly attended the hospital chapel together. In fact, they had attended the small church every day for as long as she could remember, singing hymns and praying together, often when there was no one else around. Suddenly, it became clear that the loud wailing that had become an irritating problem for her support team was really a creative personal expression and a daily routine from which she used to gain much pleasure.

The planning facilitator started to consider the hymn singing as a possible key to allowing Dee to express herself freely. So, arrangements were made for Dee's support staff to go with her to a local church and see how she got on.

At first Dee would sit at the back of the church, mainly to make a quick and unobtrusive exit if necessary because up until now she had never been able to stay in one place for any length of time. She would sing along to all the hymns and although she sang louder than many of the congregation and did not manage always to hit the right notes, she was no more out of tune than some of the other people who attended the services regularly! Certainly, no one seemed to mind, though they certainly noticed the new faces and the enthusiastic singing.

From the back of the church Dee gradually moved towards the front and became more visible as a consequence. More and more people in the congregation said hello and shook hands. More and more people would ask after Dee on the rare occasions that she was absent.

After a year or so of attending the same church, a woman who also regularly attended the Sunday morning service approached Dee one day. The woman was a member of the church choir and asked Dee if she would like to attend the choir practice on a Wednesday evening. Although Dee did not use words to communicate and seemed not to notice the offer at the time, she was thrilled when she turned up with her support worker at the midweek choir practice. People who she recognised from the church surrounded her and she was doing the thing that she loved best: she was singing with other people.

Several years have passed and there have been ups and downs with Dee and her attendance at the church. The choir has definitely benefited from their contact with Dee and her circle. Dee has had choir members coming round her house to offer lifts to the choir practice or to see if she is all right if she missed the a practice.

It is only a beginning, but the future is full of promise. With more people involved in Dee's life, the possibilities appear limitless.

In Dee's story the wailing and moaning which was a source of great irritation to staff, was redefined as her way of expressing herself, and transformed into singing when Dee joined the choir at her local church.

This quite often happens naturally. Much problem behaviour is the result of institutionalisation and disappears gradually once the person is living in the community. Other behaviour can be a result of unhappiness and changes once the person is living in a situation in which she is more content.

All of us have unique characteristics and behaviour. As adults we are able to seek out places where we feel comfortable, where people behave like us. People with disabilities have less choice about this and are often taken out to places where their support team, rather than they, feel at home.

Denise is a young woman, gifted with flamboyance. She dresses flamboyantly in bright colours, large earrings and lots of make up. She acts flamboyantly, talking a lot and loudly, embracing people she has only just met and asking direct questions.

Denise lives in a house with four other people but doesn't know many people of her own age. She wanted to meet people, so her support worker, Angie, decided to take her out. The first place they went to was the local pub. Angie is well known there because she has always lived in the area. It is a fairly quiet pub where local couples go out for a meal and tourists pop in for a drink. Angie realized within a few minutes that she had made a mistake. Denise behaved as always, laughing and joking loudly and engaging people in conversation. The trouble was that people didn't want to talk – they had come out for an intimate evening. Angie felt embarrassed and Denise realized that she wasn't welcome. They went home after about an hour, both feeling that the evening had been a failure.

The next day Angie met with her team and they considered what had gone wrong. Instead of blaming Denise for her behaviour, which has always been part of her and which makes her lovable as well as being awkward sometimes, they blamed themselves for not having thought through the issue sufficiently well. The next week Angie and Denise travelled to the local town where they went to a Goth club. Everybody there was dressed flamboyantly, the music was loud so you had to shout and people enjoyed talking with Denise. Angie has left the team now but Denise still goes to the club with a woman she met there.

It is extremely limiting to assume that behaviour has to be changed in order for people to participate in community life. There is behaviour that people can't change. Spending too much time trying to change it is frustrating and demoralising and it can become oppressive. People who have lived in hospital many years are accustomed to be being told that they cannot have something unless they achieve something else – they can't live in their own home unless they can cook a meal for themselves. No one should deny people the opportunity to meet others because they cannot or do not want to change their behaviour.

Furthermore, those working towards inclusion are not trying to change disabled people but to change society. Much of our effort should be focused on making difference acceptable rather than eliminating it.

However, practically speaking, this is a long-term goal and there is a primary duty to ensure that individuals are aware of the consequences of their behaviour and actions in the society we live in now.

4. WHAT ARE THE RISKS?

If you don't risk anything you risk even more.

Erica Jong

Life is a risky business. Meeting new people involves the risk that they might hurt us emotionally or physically. We can protect the individual from risk but only to a limited extent. We can carry out police checks – but these cost money and might put potential friends off. In any case such checks only tell us what a person has been caught doing and not what they might do. We can also take basic precautions. These could include:

- meeting the community person ourselves
- escorting the focus person to the meeting
- ensuring that the focus person and community person meet in a public place
- giving the focus person a mobile phone or pager
- enquiring after the relationship
- listening to what the focus person is telling us about the relationship and watching out for changes in behaviour
- ensuring that the focus person meets a variety of people, not just one person.

Although things rarely go wrong, the consequences are disastrous when they do, not only for the individual themselves but also for the agency and its staff and

potentially for a member of the community. Our society (and therefore our local and national politicians) and our social work departments (and therefore our support agencies) are all very intolerant of risk and it is, therefore, essential to do some form of risk assessment to ensure that we have considered as many risks as possible and done what we can to minimize them.

> As ordinary citizens we can make decisions about the risks we take in our lives. We may choose to go rock-climbing, knowing that injury is possible, but the sense of achievement makes it worthwhile. People with learning disabilities need support to achieve their personal goals. This should not mean putting them at risk but it also does not mean over-protecting them. For this to be possible, users, carers, support staff and managers need to be clear about what risks are acceptable.[61]

An example of what such a framework could look like and how it might work is outlined below.

Denise goes to the Goth club without her support worker for the first time but with a friend she has met there.

Likely

High Impact

A

D

Low Impact

C

B

E

Not Likely

Risks

A. She is too friendly and annoys people.

B. She gets separated from her friend and has to find her way back on her own.

C. She goes home with someone else and ends up in a vulnerable situation.

D. She doesn't enjoy it.

E. She drinks too much or takes drugs.

Risk A was quite likely to happen but unlikely to have much impact. Denise is a very friendly person and likely to talk to complete strangers. However people normally make it clear to Denise when she is bothering them, she doesn't mind and just talks to someone else. The team decided they didn't have to plan for that.

Risk B was unlikely to happen but could have a very high impact. The team decided to stress to Denise's friend how important it was that she stayed with her and brought her home at the end of the night. They also gave Jill a mobile phone with the 'on call' number programmed in so that she could phone if anything happened. They also programmed in a taxi phone number.

Risk C was unlikely to happen but again could have a very high impact. The team decided to talk to Denise about their concerns and to her friend to try to ensure that they came home together at the end of the night. Denise and her support worker have ongoing discussions about personal safety and sexual health.

Risk D was quite likely to happen but unlikely to have a high impact. If Denise wasn't enjoying herself she was quite capable of leaving. Because she had the mobile phone she could ring 'on call' or a taxi if she wanted to go home before her friend.

Risk E was unlikely to happen but could have a high impact. Denise never drinks too much. She normally only has a couple of beers before reverting to coke. The team discussed the possibility that someone might spike her drink but didn't think it very likely. Nevertheless they told Denise to mind out.

Denise thought her team were worrying about nothing but they felt better having discussed the possibilities and done as much as they could to protect her from unnecessary risks while supporting her freedom to live life as she chooses.

Friendship can bring pain and betrayal. This can be intensified for people with disabilities if it is one of the few friendships they have. We cannot protect individuals from emotional rejection, but we need to remember the possibility of it and support them through it.

There are risks attached to not making connections too – the risks of being permanently isolated and unloved.

Morag was introduced to her local church at a time when she needed to meet people and also to reconnect with her own spirituality. She is a woman who lives on her own in the community but has support needs in relation, among other things, to a drug problem. She immediately felt welcomed by the church. After a few months she was invited, along with two other women she knew to visit the Iona community with the church for a weekend. Morag hasn't much money so the church offered to pay. Morag wanted to go very much but was unsure how well she would manage. Her support worker talked it through with her and encouraged her to believe in herself. The weekend was well planned to be as safe as possible, her GP thought it was a good idea and the social worker was on board. The day before the trip, Morag's support worker left for her own holiday. That evening the social worker panicked and told Morag she didn't think she was up to it. Morag lost confidence and pulled out. Since then she has not been back to the church feeling that she let them down. She has trouble planning holidays now and has lost faith that she is capable.

The most authentic perspectives on risk come from individuals themselves and their loved ones. The best protection against the vagaries of life for anyone is to have a group of loving friends around them. Jeff and Cindy Strully spoke for many other parents when they said:

> It is friendship that will ultimately mean life or death for our daughter. It is her and our only hope for a desirable future and protection from victimization.[62]

Cory Moore writes:

> Life in the community does not come without risk. Even as we weigh the significant possibilities of growth, the cultivation of personal responsibility and independence, the value of integration, companionship and participation in decision making, skill development, a weaning from psychological dependence, a more normalized existence, we are still scared.[63]

Taking the Plunge

By this stage our initial strategy is usually clear. It will have been dictated by a number of factors:

- the individual's own preference about a way forward
- how much time we have

- who we are in the person's life (e.g. friend, family member, external/internal community builder, support worker) and therefore what is appropriate for us to do
- whether the individual has existing networks which could be better used
- whether we have networks we could use
- whether the individual has a burning interest which could lead to joining a local club or association
- how vibrant the local community is
- whether the individual has a passionate desire to change the world
- what we as community connectors feel comfortable with or have personal experience of
- what the risks are.

If there is still no obvious place to start, a 'brainstorming' exercise might help.

The community connector should always have the focus person's permission to do this because it involves speaking about the person whilst they are not there.

The community connector gathers a group of creative thinkers (either the team, a group of friends or a group of people the same age or background as the focus person). The connector presents a portrait of the person, emphasising her gifts, skills and hopes for future, as well as what is known about what works and doesn't work for her (in terms of people, places and activities).

Once the connector has finished describing the focus person, the other people are invited to brainstorm ideas for possible connections. The connector must write everything down without question or discussion. It is essential that the idea-generators be as imaginative and free-flowing as possible.

Afterwards the connector takes away the list and, together with the focus person, decides whether there are any ideas worth taking forward.

This approach has had very fruitful results in many teams.

A worker who was attending a course on community connecting, discovered that brainstorming could unleash a whole range of possible ideas for potential connections. Before she went on the course, she had discussed it with Owen, a man whom she supported and she had his agreement that they would work together when she returned from the course. With his permission, the worker presented a pen-portrait of Owen to a group of people who didn't know him at all. She told the group about

his likes and dislikes, his gifts, his skills and his interests. She also told them the kinds of places and activities that work for Owen and those that don't work for him. After this the group came up with a lot of ideas for making possible connections. Since no discussion was allowed of the ideas at the time, the creative energy kept flowing and a surprising number of new ideas were generated.

When she returned from the course, she discussed the ideas with Owen and asked him if any appealed to him. A lot of the ideas were dismissed straight away but the one that he really liked the sound of was to train as an ABE tutor. Owen continues the story:

'A few months ago, I saw an advert in the paper about becoming an ABE tutor. ABE stands for Adult Basic Education. The role of the ABE tutor is to teach adults who have difficulties with reading, writing and numeracy. I submitted an application form and was later called for an interview where they went over my application with me.

They then replied to me within two weeks to let me know that I had been a suitable candidate.

On my first night, I was nervous and did not know what to expect, but now I am becoming more comfortable, and have got to learn new more things, and have got to know more people.

The training I am undergoing at present involves reading a variety of different books and leaflets that helps me understand more about ABE. I feel the training I am involved in at present will be a benefit to other people, and a good experience for myself.'

In this chapter we have outlined what we need to think about before we get started. The next three chapters examine several strategies for community connecting including:

- community mapping
- using networks
- making a contribution
- work
- creating opportunities in the community.

chapter four
community mapping

A community can mean a geographical place or neighbourhood, or it can mean the people, places and associations to which we are connected. One way of learning about communities is through 'community mapping'. This helps us think about where to begin building connections. There are various times in our lives when we move from one area to another – leaving home for college, moving to a new job, or simply wanting to live somewhere else – and having done so we then need to make new connections. The ways to successfully do this are the same whoever we are and wherever we live. Community mapping is one way to understand this process of discovery. This chapter covers:

- Community mapping
- Third places
- Making connections through places
- Making connections through associations and groups
- Asking and inviting.

COMMUNITY MAPPING

Many of the ideas about community mapping in this chapter are developed from the pioneering community building work of John McKnight, in North America. Much of his theory is based on research into Logan Square, Chicago, where a deliberate community-building effort took place that focused on pooling community information and inviting people to help each other. It led to more than twenty natural relationships being developed and sustained between established community members and people living in supported accommodation in the community.

Cafe

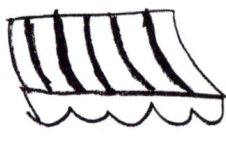

Betty, works in the cafe

Post Office

Mrs Spencer at post office
(knows everyone)

Allotments

allotments society

Houses

Mrs Smith
neighbourhood watch organizer

tea dance
mother and toddlers group
lunch club
five-a-side football
Friends of the Earth group

Community Centre

Jill, community centre manager
(very friendly)

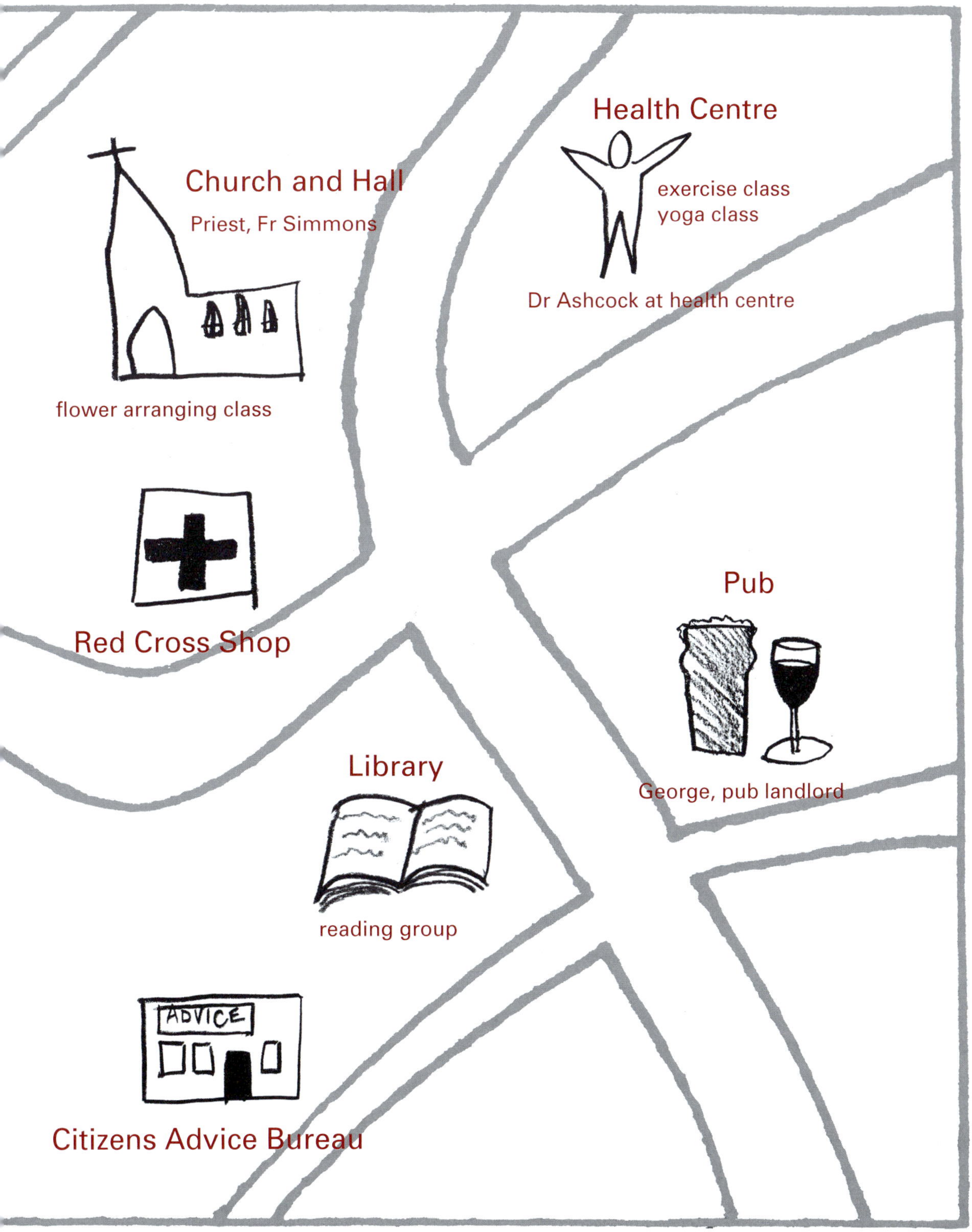
Health Centre
exercise class
yoga class
Dr Ashcock at health centre
Church and Hall
Priest, Fr Simmons
flower arranging class
Red Cross Shop
Pub
George, pub landlord
Library
reading group
ADVICE
Citizens Advice Bureau

When we think about mapping communities we can begin by gathering information about the:

- physical features
- organizations
- people
- opportunities for which people would travel further
- characteristics of the local community.

Physical features: facilities, shops, leisure centres, employment, education, health, banks, council services, places of worship, places to eat and drink.

Organizations: work; leisure, e.g. supporters clubs, amateur dramatics; hobbies, e.g. collectors groups, stamps, memorabilia; interests, e.g. health and fitness; religious; political; charity, e.g. St Johns Ambulance; voluntary, e.g. senior citizen groups; cultural, e.g. local history, African-Caribbean.

People: chairs and directors of organizations and community groups; people with particular roles, e.g. doctor's receptionist, postwoman/man, faith leaders; people with community knowledge, e.g. police officer, community education workers; well-connected community figures, e.g. celebrities and particular councillors; campaigners /lobbyists, e.g. those featured in local papers etc.

Opportunities for which people often travel further: e.g. into the city for theatres, museums, galleries, events; into the country for stately houses, parks.

Characteristics of a community: e.g. traditions of hospitality – how does the community welcome strangers? What are the 'social rules and expectations' that we need to know to 'fit in'?

Developing a community map

The best way to gather this information, wherever possible, is with the individuals themselves. Using local libraries, local newspapers, Yellow Pages, the Internet, information centres and talking to local people are often the best places to start. You could put a request out on a community website at a local cybercafe. It can be a bit like doing private detective work – finding things out and following what may initially look like unpromising leads. Chance encounters with different people whilst out shopping or in the leisure centre can sometimes provide surprisingly useful information. This means that we need to constantly keep our eyes open for opportunities. We need to pay attention to people from different ethnic backgrounds and their involvement in and contribution to the local community.

Community mapping can be time-consuming and it is sensible to get together with other people who may already be doing it in other projects or services nearby.

The focus person should direct the operation of community mapping as far as possible. Rather than collecting information on absolutely everything, the community map should focus on the individual's interests; what she wants to contribute, and her ideas for other activities or experiences she would like to try. It is important to record information in a way that is accessible for the person, for example drawing a plan of the streets and placing items on it, or a photo or video diary about the different places.

James, who lives in a group home in a small fishing community in the North of Scotland, took on the task of community mapping for himself. With the help of his keyworker, he gathered information from all the resources in the community and created a folder in which to keep it all. He has put his name on to all sorts of mailing lists, so that he receives information as it is published and he makes it his job to go round the community collecting up-to-date information about what's on in the area. Consequently, he now has a respected role in the house as the person in the know. If anyone wants to know what is on at the theatre or what time the swimming pool opens, they only need to knock on James' door and he is very happy to help. In doing this, he has also got to know lots more people in the community, as well as finding out about a few clubs that he wanted to join himself.

A project manager recounts how one small group-home went about using their local community and overcoming initial hostility.

Despite strong opposition in the initial stages of planning and development for the house, since the service started, the local community has been extremely supportive.

No doubt the environment helped tenants to 'settle in'. It's a small town and although this can sometimes mean there is less privacy, it does also mean that people quickly get to know and recognise one another. The response from the 'person in the street' on a day-to-day level has always been good. The fears, which were initially expressed, seem to have dissipated.

Our house is newly built and opened coincidentally with other buildings, which are identical – we are therefore not intruding on territory which belonged to others – our immediate neighbours moved in at the same time.

On a day-to-day basis, people living in the home have used local resources such as the shops and banks, and have therefore provided trade in the local area. We are recognised and greeted like other people who get their pint of milk in the morning.

It is important to be proactive in the community when out and about – if we pass someone in the street we say hello and we always chat to local shopkeepers and neighbours. We hosted the meeting for the housing association and went out of our way to make the occasion informal and enjoyable by providing a buffet and drinks.

We have found it extremely helpful to tackle the community on an individual basis. When the house first opened we took surplus sandwiches and cakes from our Open Day to a nearby Nursing Home as a gesture of good will. The folks there enjoyed a chat and will hopefully tell their families positive things about us. As a result our links with them have been good and led to voluntary work for one tenant.

Our house has certainly benefited from a mixture of staff, including people who have lived locally for some time. Familiar faces can help to break down barriers. In addition, it's always handy to know people who can access services through 'word of mouth'. Through this we have used local facilities to produce posters for functions, as training venues and for transport. We have also gained access to infor- mal services through friends of local staff such as a local man who leads walks for tenants in the nearby park.

Moving into a small town and getting known has worked well for us. We have been approached by someone wishing to volunteer as a befriender. He is a local man and we hope that his connections and knowledge will not only be a fresh perspective, but will also provide further avenues for inclusion. We can view initial points of contact, from a brief hello in the street through to involving locals in Mental Health Awareness week (through a craft fair and shop) as a pyramid – I speak to one person, that person speaks to their friends and so on.

Above all staff should be encouraged to have a positive attitude when advocating for tenants and approaching community members – this often means making the first move, and taking those first friendly steps, but the dividends are great and have a real impact on the opportunities available for inclusion.[64]

This story emphasises the prime importance of getting to know the neighbours. This can serve both to allay any prejudice or fear and could also turn out to be a useful connection.

Finding 'bridge-builders'

Sharon enlisted Francis to act as a 'bridge-builder'. Francis is a long time leader of local associations from the town's marching band to a food pantry for the town's many unemployed industrial workers. She asked him, as an expert in community life, to introduce previously excluded people to community associations that will benefit from their contribution.[65]

There might be natural bridge-builders in a particular area. They could be someone with a particular role in the area, such as a community councillor or minister or they could be someone who just knows everyone. Often they are people who have lived in the area a long time or who have been involved in lots of community activities.

Jo's neighbour, Edna, is one such person. She has lived in the same city for fifteen years. She makes curtains and upholstery and used to run a shop. She campaigns for a local political party and has recently been active in a community campaign to stop a mobile phone mast being erected on the church. When she moved into her new house, she introduced herself to all the neighbours and invited them round for a drink. She has a dog and walks it locally where she meets other dog-walkers. Whenever Jo needs to know something she asks Edna and if Jo were trying to introduce someone to a neighbourhood Edna would be an ideal person to turn to.

The advantage of natural bridge-builders is that they already know the area and are trusted by the community. Sometimes it helps just to get them on board, even if they are not going to be asked to do anything specific. For example, an organization based in a small community in Scotland, established some very useful links with key members of that community. The organization aimed to support people with learning difficulties to build-up links in the community and it helped to have the support of local people. These people didn't come together in any formal way, but agreed to be called upon for information and contacts. Sometimes, this is called building a Trust Network Database.

DISCOVERING 'THIRD PLACES'

Third places are those places in a community where locals gather to chat and be together. These are great places to help people become part of the

neighbourhood and to find out who in the community is a natural 'connector'. Cafés, pubs, community centres, leisure centres and Post Offices are all likely third places.

Ray Oldenburg describes third places as having certain characteristics:[66]

- They can feel like a home away from home – people feel rooted and see familiar faces.
- The mood is playful – there is laughter, people are having a good time.
- They have a low profile – the place is typically plain, often unimpressive and therefore does not attract lots of strangers.
- There are regulars – on any visit someone will see someone they know.
- Conversation is the main activity.
- They act as a leveller – a place that is inclusive, accessible and does not have formal membership.
- They are on neutral ground – people come and go; no one is 'host'.

A third place could be a café:

George lives on his own in a big city. He enjoys going out locally with his support workers and he started going regularly to the local café. Very soon they began to be recognised there. It's a small place where people all know one another. When George goes there people greet him and ask him how he is doing. He's just another regular. A few weeks ago, a staff member, Liz went to the café with someone else, and George was already there. They went to sit with George and Liz was immediately struck by how many people he knew. When she was paying she asked the man who owns the café if he needed any staff and when he replied that he was looking for someone to work at weekends, Liz said that George might be looking for a job. The owner said that he would insist on paying him properly for his time. George is thinking about it and his staff team are reluctant. They think that the café is full of drug users at weekends and George could be at risk. But it is a place where George feels at home and where he is fully accepted for who he is. The staff team need to think about how they can support him and minimize the risks, so that he can make the most of the opportunities that he has created for himself out of his own sociability.

Or a church:

Jessie is the minister of a church in a small town. Since the closure of a hospital nearby several people with learning disabilities have moved back into the area. Some of them come along to the church. Lisbeth sits at the front of the church and

occasionally she mutters swear words in an audible whisper. Jessie, at the altar, is more disconcerted than those sitting around Lisbeth who appear to concentrate on their prayers. Jeff greets everyone he meets and people speak to him because he is so engaging. At communion he compliments the person giving it to him, saying, 'This is lovely tasting wine'. He turns formal occasions on their heads and everyone enjoys it. Two members of the congregation (both support staff who come along in their own right) help to include people.. One is good at challenging attitudes and the other helps community members feel more comfortable, when necessary, by explaining the way that some individuals communicate. Of their efforts, Jessie says that the congregation 'doesn't think about it, and therefore they do it well'. It is an old community and people don't move very often. In the old days people who were different weren't taken away and the community still retains a strong sense of look-ing after their own. Now the congregation is growing in confidence. people don't just greet Lisbeth and Jeff in church; they have begun to invite them to parties.

Using a community map to lead to connections

Once you know what the person is interested in, and what is available in the community, the next step is to start making connections by actually introducing the person to an activity, place or organization.

This is the point where things start to come together: the information from the person's portfolio, the work on the introduction and the contract, as well as all the community mapping information.

It may be helpful to summarise what you have gathered so far in a checklist:

Skills and interests, qualities and identities, we hope to develop	Local opportunities, settings, networks and places	Contribution or roles for person within the network
I like to watch other people. I like chatty people.	Local pub or coffee shop	Customer, regular
I'm a calypso music lover	Local carnival, community centre, church choir	Local activist, group member, choir member
I really like animals, especially dogs	PDSA, RSPCA, local pet store	Dog walker, trainer, volunteer

There are several ways of making connections, including:

- connecting people through being in the same place in the community
- connecting people by joining clubs and associations.

CONNECTING PEOPLE THROUGH PLACES IN THE COMMUNITY

We make friends with people we're around a lot. Sociologists have shown that proximity or physical closeness is the number one factor affecting who we make friends with. We are more likely to develop a close friendship with our next-door neighbour or someone we work with every day than with someone we only bump into occasionally.[67]

The first step to connecting people is obvious – people need to be living, working and spending their free time with other people in their community. Fundamental to this is a focus on opportunities for relationships rather than just on activities. Some activities have a greater possibility than others that the person will meet and get to know new people. Agencies are trying harder to enable people they support to get out and about – sometimes they can try too hard. Individuals can feel that they never have a chance to relax. They may also spend much of their time doing things where they are unlikely to meet others. An outing to a shopping centre or a cinema is unlikely to produce an opportunity to get to know people – shopping centres make good places for 'people watching' but are less effective for 'people meeting'.

Going to the same café at the same time on a regular basis would create a familiarity that could lead to new relationships. There would be more chance of this happening if the person went with someone who was already a 'regular'. Therefore, when starting to help people make connections, we need to consider not only the activity, but also its opportunities for meeting people.

Michelle loves swimming. Every week she goes to Musselburgh pool, with her support worker, Tracy, as she has for the past few years. When she first started going there, the manageress was very helpful and that helped them to get settled in to using the pool. Over time, Michelle has got to know a lot of the other regulars. Tracy is Michelle's one-to-one worker for thirty hours a week, but when they go swimming Michelle needs two people to help her to get in and out of the water. Usually, another worker goes along, but sometimes, if there isn't another worker available, one of the women from the pool helps out.

When Michelle was looking for somewhere to have her weekly physio sessions, the leisure centre seemed an obvious place. The manageress was very open to the idea and Michelle has been having her physio in the pulse centre every Friday for a few years now. She is allowed to store her equipment there. There was hesitation from the physiotherapy department, but Michelle's own physiotherapist, who knew her well, was keen to give it a go and it's worked really well ever since.

The leisure centre is very important in Michelle's life. Going there each week at the same time on Tuesdays and Fridays has meant that she has got to know lots of people, who stop to chat with her. It's a friendly place – not too big and very welcoming. It's quite a long way from where Michelle lives, but other people from her local community go there to use the facilities too.

The women Michelle knows at the swimming pool stepped in to help with fundraising for a car for Michelle. They heard that Tracy and Michelle were organising a 'Stars in Their Eyes' social, so they tapped on the changing room door and asked for tickets. Then they took it upon themselves to organize a fundraiser, selling raffle tickets at the pool and putting on an exhibition. One man from the pool even raised money by running a half-marathon. Together, they successfully raised enough money for Michelle to buy a fully-adapted Mercedes van, which has allowed Michelle to make use of community facilities even more. It means she can visit people, like her Gran, more regularly. She can go out to more places more easily and she doesn't have to hang around waiting for transport.

Tracy believes it helps that Michelle is such a chatty person herself, despite not using words. Tracy helps people to feel comfortable with her, showing them by her own example how to talk to Michelle. Tracy thinks that people will be friendly if they are shown 'how to be', even though people are often scared or embarrassed at first.

CONNECTING PEOPLE THROUGH CLUBS AND ASSOCIATIONS

Three years ago Jesse took a job as a supportive flatmate for James. They get on very well. Jesse plays the fiddle and every Tuesday evening he goes to the local folk club for a jam session with fifteen to twenty other people. James goes with him. He loves it there. Jesse introduced him to his friends and now everyone knows him and welcomes him. Now he doesn't bother taking staff with him anymore, he just gets a beer and sits down with the musicians.

Occasionally just being there is enough and opportunities come along, but usually we have to be more proactive about it. People who work in services

often have reservations about this, thinking that they are being pushy, or that it feels 'unnatural'.

'Invitation lies at the heart of community building and shapes the responses people offer.' [68]

If the chosen activity involves joining a club or group, there are three possible options. Together, the focus person and the community connector will need to decide:

- whether the community connector is also going to join the group as a member
- whether the community connector needs to go along in the background to support the person
- whether they should invite someone else to get involved in supporting the person at the group (either someone already known to the person or someone identified within the group).

Once the focus person has identified a club or group that she is interested in exploring, the next stage is to find out as much about the club as possible, so that she can plan how to get involved.

Every group has its own characteristics, social rules, expectations and demands, and time should be taken to work out what these are. How, for example, do people usually dress? How are strangers welcomed? It will be much easier to 'fit in' with a group if effort is made to follow these rules and expectations. People supporting individuals to make connections will need to model these rules and think about how to communicate them to the individuals they are seeking to connect.

Here is a list that might help to get started:[69]

The Stages of Interaction

Arrival: List things related to how people arrive at the group or place.

Entry: List the things related to how people actually get into the building or location. Do people have to walk up stairs, knock, or open a door?

Getting started: List anything that happens from the point that you get into the building until the activity actually starts. This could be finding a seat, knowing to be quiet when the meeting begins, greeting other people, introducing yourself etc. Sometimes, the atmosphere is very relaxed while other situations have more formality. Are there any unwritten rules?

Participation: List anything that occurs during the main portion of the situation or meeting. This can vary greatly. Look for unwritten rules, types of interaction, types of conversation, as well as 'things' that are required, for example, if you were going to a café, you'd need to take some money.

Finishing up: How can you tell that the activity is winding down? Are there specific things that occur? Again, remember the unwritten rules.

Exit: List whatever is required to leave the building. Pay attention to whether people talk with one another on the way out, whether people go out for coffee after the activity etc.

Characteristics: A running description of anything relevant that occurs at particular stages – things like how people are dressed, seating arrangements, or anything else that seems relevant given the setting and the person you will be supporting.

Expectations and demands: Includes anything that the setting demands during a particular stage. It could be a response such as shaking hands, collecting music books etc.

Describe the people who are part of the setting: This can include a variety of things such as age, gender, 'type' of person, and how people dress, anything that strikes you as relevant or defining about the group.

Community members will learn from support staff the best ways to behave with the focus person. If they see individuals being treated respectfully then it is more likely that they will also treat them with respect; if they see individuals being talked about as if they were not there then community members will learn that it is alright to treat people as if they are invisible. We need to remember that we teach by example.

Social codes within groups are not set in stone. They change and adapt to suit the people involved in the group. Initially, it will be necessary to fit in with the current social rules, but over time each person makes their own mark.

When David started attending his local church, he used to sit at the back. Over time he noticed that other regular churchgoers had their own pew, which they sat in every week. At first, David felt that he didn't want to be noticed and he would slip in just before the service began and leave as soon as the last hymn was sung. Over time, however, as people started to recognise him and welcome him and be less put off by his large and loud presence, David felt confident enough to stay for coffee after the service. He also decided that he would like to have a regular pew and he chose to sit near the back and to the left, near enough to leave if he wanted to and close to the toilet. The church welcomed this and from then on left his pew empty for him to go in to. After he had been attending the church for a few years, he was asked if he wanted to take on the role of handing out the hymnbooks so that he could chat to people as they came in for the Sunday service.

Finally, if an organization is receptive to including one person with disabilities, it doesn't necessarily mean it will, or should, be equally receptive to others. People need to be treated individually and organizations or associations need to be found which suit them.

This chapter has described how to find out about your community through community mapping. Mapping is more than just listing the places in the community that you may use, it is also about discovering who the significant people are who 'know everyone' and what the local groups, clubs and associations are. Once you have this information you can match the themes that you discovered from making the portfolio described in the previous chapter, to local opportunities. This may produce a plan to try and connect the focus person via sharing community places, or joining a new group or association. The next chapter describes a different approach – using our own networks.

chapter five
networks

We start building networks for ourselves from the moment we go out into the world. At nursery school we develop a group of friends that changes and grows throughout school and college. We take our networks of old friends and family with us from job to job and house to house. We also build new networks in our geographical communities and in our workplaces.

We use these networks in many different ways: to help with childcare; to provide a shoulder to cry on; to seek advice; to find work; to borrow money; to celebrate with. In turn, we use our networks to meet other people. So, we meet partners through friends or colleagues; we might ask a friend to recommend a plumber or a hairdresser; we join clubs that our friends belong to, and so on.

We have already looked at why people with disabilities have less opportunity to develop networks. Some people are completely isolated; a few have good strong networks; others only have very limited networks consisting of people who are paid to be in their lives and other people who use the same services.

In this chapter we will examine how we can use existing networks to enable people to make connections. In particular, we will look at:

- using the focus person's own network
- using our own network
- trust networks

- networking skills
- Circles of Support
- citizen advocacy

USING THE FOCUS PERSON'S OWN NETWORK

One of the first things we need to ascertain when starting to help individuals think about making community connections is who they already know. We can do this through talking with them and drawing up a relationship map (as described in Chapter Two). They may want to see the people they already know more regularly, to rekindle old relationships, or to get to know new people.

This initial step of relationship mapping can have immediate results:

My name is Roberta and I have lived in a group home in Fraserburgh for eighteen years. My friend Christine lives in Perth; we used to visit each other on holiday then lost touch for several years.

Last summer my keyworker contacted Christine and arranged an outing; we met at Aberdeen bus station then had a picnic at Haddo House, followed by strawberries and ice cream. It was lovely to see my friend again and catch-up with what had been happening since we last met.

I read in our organization's newsletter that Christine is moving on to a satellite house so I'm sure we will have lots to talk about at our next reunion.

Friends and family often have strong social networks that could potentially (and often do) include the focus person. Friends and family may feel that they want to help but don't know how to start. On the other hand they may also feel that they have no place in providing support to the focus person. McKnight[70] and Schwarz[71] both demonstrate the ways in which services have excluded families for many years to such an extent that families often feel that the focus person needs professional support in all aspects of their lives and that they, as friends and family with no professional qualifications, have nothing to offer. The role of community connector can be to support family and friends to take up their natural roles again, as we can see in Dave's story.

Dave's story

Dave lives in a group home with three other people. He is warm and friendly, and although he doesn't use words to speak, he can make his views known. Dave has

a big heart and is well liked by staff and loved by his family. Dave's father and brother visit him regularly. His mother is dead but her best friend, Jean, is almost part of the family.

Jean knows everyone in Dave's neighbourhood. She has lived and worked there all her life. Whenever Dave goes down to the pub with a member of staff they always see someone Jean knows. Dave's staff team members, knowing how sociable he is, were keen to provide him with more opportunities to meet people. Together with Dave, they decided to have a meeting to think about this. Dave invited his Dad, his brother and Jean along with his support team and Bill, who used to work with him.

People had lots of ideas about things Dave could do. One was dog-walking because Dave likes dogs. This was successful and Dave got to know a couple of people who lived nearby through walking their dogs for them.

However, the team knew that the best way for Dave to meet people was through Jean. Although she was wholehearted in her love for Dave and could see that he needed more people in his life, she was nervous that people would take advantage of him or mock him. The meeting was the first step in introducing her to the idea that Dave wanted to get to know more people, and indeed, that Dave could contribute to his local community. The team decided to spend some time supporting Jean to feel happier and safer about Dave going out more and to devise ways of minimising the risk to him emotionally and physically. They could see that, once Jean felt more comfortable, she could include him in her circle.

Lindsay's story illustrates how her support team asked a member of her family for help.

Lindsay's story

Lindsay loves newspapers. Before her accident she had a job selling them. Lindsay is close to her support team and has a strong relationship with her sister. She likes being with people on a one-to-one basis and finds it hard to share the attention of staff and family. Lindsay's support team are anxious to give her the opportunity to come into contact with other people in the hope that she might one day want to widen her network. They contacted her sister who works in a garage and asked whether it would be possible for Lindsay to work with her when she was on shift. Her sister, Wendy, was quite happy and agreed to support Lindsay to do this. Lindsay now works in the garage. She also has a job in a charity shop and goes to

the gym. The next step is building relationships. Lindsay does not feel the need to do that at the moment but she is in the right places for them to happen. Alice's story shows how someone can take on the task for themselves of organizing their family and friends to support them more effectively.

Alice's story

Alice lives in her own home. She is hospitable, outgoing, gregarious and fun to be with. She has a close family and lots of friends. Leaving the house is sometimes difficult for her and she is anxious about going on public transport on her own. Sometimes she has periods of bad health, both physical and mental, and she ends up being admitted into hospital.

After one such admission, Alice decided that she didn't want to be admitted to hospital on mental health grounds again. With the help of her support worker she undertook an essential lifestyle plan. Alice drew up the plan herself, interviewing her family and friends about what they liked about her and what they thought was non-negotiable in her life. The process of drawing up the plan allowed her to discuss things with her family and friends, which she had never discussed before, such as what helped her and what didn't help her.

Once she had drawn up most of the plan she decided to have a meeting. Everyone she had interviewed was invited. Everyone brought food and drink and in the end twelve people were crammed into the living room of her flat. The meeting focused on how her family and friends could support her never to go to hospital again. She told them about how they could tell when she was getting near to breaking point – she spends a lot of money; her flat becomes messy. At that point if they stayed with her and supported her, even if she didn't directly ask for it, they could keep her safe. She pointed out the things that were likely to upset her – arriving late without phoning, getting angry on the phone.

The meeting wasn't all one way. Alice's friends and family also talked about what they found hard to deal with and Alice listened. A few months after the meeting, Alice became unwell again. The people who had been at the meeting drew up a rota between themselves and stayed at her house for two weeks to keep her out of hospital. Since then they have done it twice more but because her family and friends now know how to help her, Alice has not been back to hospital.

These stories all illustrate how an individual's friends and family can be crucial in supporting her and in introducing her to new people and opportunities.

USING OUR OWN NETWORKS

The best and most natural way of connecting individuals is to make use of their existing networks. Unfortunately, many people with disabilities do not have good networks. Where this is the case, it may be possible for community connectors to use their own networks to help get individuals started.

They are different ways of using our own networks. We need to examine:

- what the networks are
- how we might use them
- how we feel about using them.

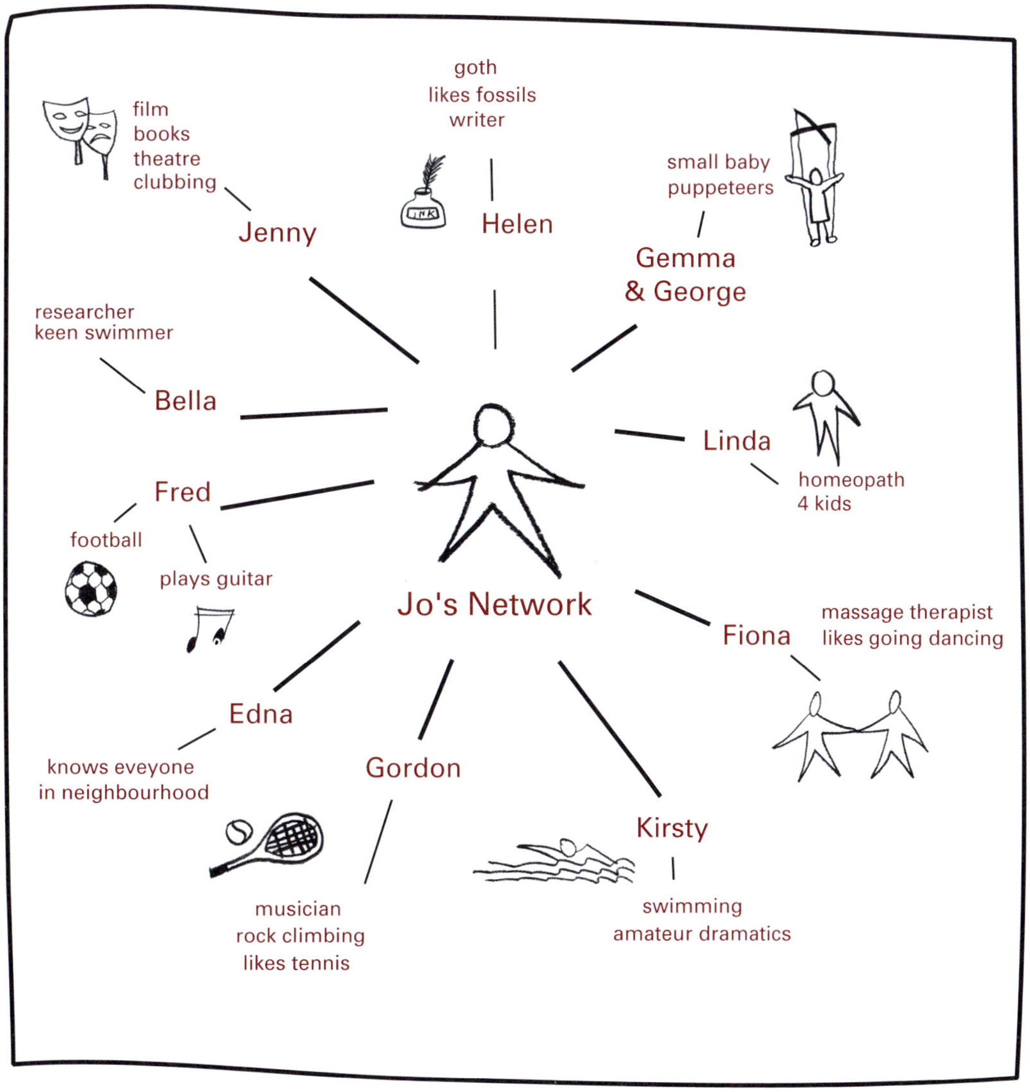

goth
likes fossils
writer

film
books
theatre
clubbing

Jenny

Helen

small baby
puppeteers

Gemma
& George

researcher
keen swimmer

Bella

Linda

homeopath
4 kids

Fred

football

plays guitar

Jo's Network

massage therapist
likes going dancing

Fiona

Edna

knows eveyone
in neighbourhood

Gordon

Kirsty

musician
rock climbing
likes tennis

swimming
amateur dramatics

It is invariably true that once we start the work of community connecting, we do start to see our own networks differently. We become very interested in how we meet people; we may start feeling that we do not do enough to get to know our neighbours; we start looking at our friends in the light of what they do and the networks they have access to.

We can use our networks in different ways. They can provide a direct match:

I went on a three-day inclusion course. On the second day we were set a task: make a connection between someone we know and someone we work with, based on a shared interest.

I was really hoping for a connection for someone I was keyworker for, but instead I realised that my partner, Bruce, loves to play snooker but rarely has anyone to play with, while my keyperson's partner, Steve, also played snooker but only ever with his keyworker.

I went home and asked Bruce if he would be interested in playing snooker with Steve. He had met Steve briefly and he readily agreed. Then I asked Steve – he was keen too. I had made the connection!

That was nearly two years ago. Every so often one guy phones the other and they go and have a game of snooker. It seems to suit them and they have continued to meet although I have changed my job and no longer see Steve or his partner.

Or we can use them more indirectly.

My name is James and I live in a group home in the North of Scotland. I have two zebra finches called Chirpy and Cheep. I enjoy talking to my birds and often sit beside them while they hop about in their cage and chirp to me.

I didn't know how to look after them properly so borrowed books from the library – when Cheep laid an egg, staff almost did the same, as no one knew what to do next!

However, my keyworker told me that the Manager of the house knew Ricky, a volunteer at daycare, who attended a bird club … We got connecting!

Ricky visited and gave me a nest for Cheep to lay her eggs in; he advised me to buy nesting material. Sadly, when hatched, the baby finch only survived a few days. I now attend the Caged Birds Club on the first Wednesday of every month where I enjoy chatting to other bird owners.

Ricky helped me to complete registration forms to enter my finches in the annual bird show. Chirpy and Cheep won 1st and Special Prize rosettes. I received a trophy.

I pinned the rosettes on Chirpy and Cheep's cage - they were very proud – and so was I.

One support worker has talked about how much two people he supports enjoy coming to his house and meeting his wife and child. If workers use their own networks they need to think about how comfortable they feel with introducing people they support into their lives. People have widely differing opinions on this. For some people work is work and home is home, whereas others have a far more flexible approach.

In Chapter One we looked at the difference between friends and paid workers, and the tensions that can arise from stepping beyond traditional boundaries. If workers start a friendship with an individual or use their own networks to connect the focus person they need to ensure that:

- the connection is real – that it is based on shared interests or a genuine feeling for one another
- we don't end up feeling like we are working all the time
- we take steps to keep ourselves and the focus person as safe as possible both physically and emotionally, i.e. asking the friend and the focus person not to discuss us; letting the friend know that the focus person is on medication and shouldn't drink too much, etc.
- we talk to our team and manager about what we are doing
- we check up to see how things are going, offering support to both people involved, without seeking to interfere in the friendship.

This last point is crucial if the friendship is going to last. Friendships often hit rocky patches and it may be that the person who made the initial introduction can help the two new friends to work through this, should difficulties arise. There will often be a honeymoon period when things seem to be going so well that the 'connector' steps away completely. It is then very difficult for them to get involved if things flounder. The connector should keep an eye on things, from a distance, and make it clear that they are still available if either party needs support with the new friendship.

TRUST NETWORKS

Sometimes it may be that we can connect people through each other's networks. Some teams set up a treasure chest pooling their networks to use as a resource. It is essential that no one uses anyone else's contact without permission, and we need to be careful not to use the same people too much.

Agencies can perform the same function. An arts agency in Edinburgh links people with an interest in the arts with disabled people share that interest. They can then go to classes or performances together. It is possible to do this through large organizations asking employees what their interests are and whether they would be willing to share them. If so they can be matched up with a focus person with the same interest.

Lurking

Tom Kohler tells us to '*be always lurking, swimming quietly through the shoals of citizens*'. 'Lurking' can produce serendipitous results. The following are examples of community connectors seizing opportunities:

Jill went down to the housing office to try to sort out a problem for one of the tenants in the house where she worked. Whilst there, she got talking to one of the housing officers, Ian, and explained her job. He said that he would be interested in helping out if there was anything he could do. Jill thought about what he had said in relation to George, another tenant about the same age as the housing officer. For some time George's team had been trying to find things for him to do and ways for him to be more involved in his community. George had started numerous adult education classes at his own request, but he always dropped out after a while. Jill decided to introduce George and Ian and to see if Ian wanted to accompany George to the latest class he had signed up for, astronomy. Ian was happy to, he and George got on well and it turned out that George and Ian had grown up in the same village. Their mothers still knew each other. George didn't drop out of the astronomy class, he enjoyed going with Ian.

Isabel shared a house with Maureen, who died tragically and suddenly. Maureen's mother, Mrs Jones, had been a regular visitor to the house before her death and had got to know Isabel quite well. In the aftermath of Maureen's death her support worker was to keen to offer what support she could to Mrs Jones. She was also aware that the connection was an important one for Isabel, who had no other natural supports. She asked Mrs Jones if she would like to act as an advocate for Isabel. Mrs

Jones was keen to keep in touch but had had enough of going to meetings and reviews for her daughter. Instead she and Isabel have become firm friends and Isabel often goes to visit her at home.

Networking skills

All of the networking approaches identified above rely to some extent on the skills of the networker. As we have already said, some people are born with these skills, whereas others have to work a bit harder at them.

Jane had a job in London supporting people with learning disabilities to find employment. She herself had lived in the area for over ten years and in that time had had many different jobs, from being a market trader to a journalist, with brief spells as a cleaner and a gardener in between! So, she had a huge network of her own to draw on. She was comfortable about using it in her work and she was able to help several people to find jobs by using her own networks.

Humour, humility and courage are the key characteristics of a good networker. John McKnight uses the term 'community guide' to describe a skilled networker and further identifies six main qualities that they should possess:

1. They must have the ability to easily see the gifts people have or what their contribution might be.
2. They should be well connected. They are likely to know a lot of people personally and know of many others by name or reputation.
3. They are people who are trusted by other people.
4. They are people with a strong belief that the community is hospitable and are skilled at being hard to refuse!
5. They know that they are guides only and that their job is not to be the person's permanent escort or friend.[72]

CIRCLES OF SUPPORT

A Circle of Support is a group of people who gather round an individual to support her to make decisions about her life and then help take those decisions forward. The focus person decides who to invite into her circle. Every circle is different, because every individual is different. Some circles start small and grow much larger as new people get invited in. Others start small and stay small. Some circles have long periods when they are not used by the focus person but are re-activated at a time of crisis or decision making, while others meet regularly

for years. Most circles are close-knit groups of people, who meet informally with a common purpose around one individual. They may involve professionals but are not dominated by them.

Circles sometimes emerge out of the meeting of an existing network, as Alice's did. Most of the time one or two people found them. Commitment is needed to start a circle, initially from one or two people who are standing by the focus person, but soon from everyone involved in the circle. Someone needs to take on the role of facilitator, at least at the first few circle meetings, so that the circle gets off the ground.

When circles work well they can provide a fast and safe track to inclusion, occasionally they can work miracles.

Daphne is in her early thirties, and very outgoing. She has some support from staff but not all the time. At times when she was not being supported Daphne would often take herself to the hospital saying she had a broken leg or some other complaint. Liz thought that she might like a circle of support and asked her about it. Daphne was very keen on the idea but had no one to ask in to her circle. Liz asked one of her support team who invited five of her own relatives and friends. Daphne threw a party for them so that by the time Liz arrived to facilitate the first circle meeting they were all quite merry.

Liz immediately noticed a young woman, Brenda, who was used to chairing meetings and asked her to co-facilitate. The meeting went well because everyone was really enjoying themselves. Daphne talked about wanting to drive a car and get married. Some people present weren't sure what they would have to offer but Liz helped them to see what they could contribute. One woman was a member of a knitting club and, she invited Daphne to go along with her. Daphne has met lots of new friends through that.

After a couple of meetings Liz pulled out, leaving Brenda to facilitate. Since then the circle has doubled in size. It has raised £1000 for a holiday for Daphne, accompanied her to visit her clan in the North of Scotland, gone go-karting with her as a preparation for learning to drive and thrown a 'wedding party' in which everyone dressed up. Daphne is delighted with the effect it has had on her life and is too busy to visit the hospital anymore.

However, because circles take time to root and require commitment from everyone involved, they can be difficult to get going and many don't take off.

Jo wanted to start a circle for Lena, a woman in her sixties who was very isolated. Lena has two children in their late teens, but they rarely see their mum. Jo's hope for the circle would be that it would help Lena's daughter, Marie, to reconnect with her mother in a supportive environment. Nervous that Marie wouldn't commit to a circle, Jo asked her to come to a tea party for her mother. Marie was confused by this invitation and assumed that Jo was going to ask her to take her mother home for good. She arrived at the tea party flustered and upset and it took time to explain to her that she wasn't expected to care for her mother in that way. Although the situation was clarified, Marie refused to come to another meeting, so the circle had failed to achieve its central aim. From this Jo learnt the meaning of Kathryn Mazak's maxim 'clearly frame and fearlessly pose'.[73] Ultimately, the outcome may have been the same, but if Jo had been clear about her intentions from the start and stated them, at least confusion and upset would have been avoided.

When circles don't work it can be because:

- there is no clarity about what is happening
- no one is facilitating the process
- there is not enough commitment among circle members
- the focus person is uncomfortable about people meeting to talk about her
- there is no focus to the meetings – so nothing actually happens and people drift away
- people might have different opinions about what is right for the person and no agreed way forward can be found
- people have been invited who don't know the person well enough to feel able to commit
- people do not take on specific action steps or tasks, so they feel redundant
- the focus person is not supported to control the meeting for herself so she loses interest
- they are service-led rather than person-led.

Reflecting on her experience with support circles, Beth Mount identifies ten conditions associated with significant change. These conditions describe a support circle with a good chance of making a positive difference in the quality of a person's life.[74]

- The focus person wants a change and agrees to work with a circle of support; support circles can't be forced on people.
- All of the circle members, including the focus person, attend to the person's

capacities and gifts and search for opportunities rather than dwelling on disabilities, deficiencies and barriers.

- Circle members have chances to find out about new possibilities and new ways to organize the assistance the focus person needs.
- The circle shares a clear vision of a different life for the focus person, and the vision vividly defines the kind of opportunities the focus person needs to share unique gifts and pursue individual interests.
- At least one circle member has a strong commitment to act vigorously on the focus person's behalf.
- At least one circle member has a broad network in the focus person's local community and the skill and desire to help her build ties to other people.
- A skilled facilitator is available to the support circle.
- Some support circle members are active in organizations and coalitions aimed at changing unjust or ineffective policies.
- Some circle members develop influence with those who make policy and administer human service programmes that affect the quality of the focus person's life.
- At least one human service programme that the focus person relies on has an explicit commitment to continuous improvement in its ability to support people's full participation in community life.

CITIZEN ADVOCACY

A valued citizen who is unpaid and independent of human services creates a relationship with an individual who is at risk of social exclusion. She chooses one or several of many ways to understand, respond to and represent that individual's interests as if they were the advocate's own thus bringing their partner's gifts and concerns into circles of ordinary community life.

Citizen advocacy is a formal process for introducing respected and valued people into the lives of disabled individuals. It is organized from outwith the service system and recruits advocates from outwith services. The role of citizen advocate is unpaid and the relationship between a citizen advocate and her partner is an informal one.

Although an advocate's main task is to represent people's interests in whatever way necessary, she may also widen their networks and introduce them into community. Citizen advocacy agencies match volunteers with individuals who need advocates.

Doreen is married with two children and works as a secretary for an engineering firm. She has been Donald's citizen advocate for twelve years. She was first introduced to him through a citizen advocacy project when Donald was living in a locked ward in a long-stay hospital. He could not speak and had a label of 'profound learning disability and challenging behaviour'.

The project provided some initial training and made sure Doreen and Donald were happy with the partnership. Since then they have become an important part of each other's lives. Donald has spent weekends and holidays with Doreen, her family and friends. Doreen has assisted Donald in difficult times, like accompanying him to the general hospital for an operation and ensuring that staff who did not know him paid attention to his needs. She has helped him move to his own flat in the local community. Doreen has also helped Donald to become more confident and self-assured by showing him that he matters.

In this chapter we have explored how we can use the focus person's networks more effectively. We have considered using our own networks and the impact that this might have on our lives. We have looked at trust networks and circles of support as ways of using other peoples' networks and connecting quickly.

In the next chapter we move on from a direct examination of how we use networks to alternative strategies for making connections, including:

- finding a job
- volunteering
- making a contribution
- creating opportunities.

However, in adopting any of these alternative strategies we may still find ourselves using networks and in particular our networking skills.

chapter six
making a contribution

Citizenship can be defined as '*the state of being or of having rights and duties of a citizen; conduct in relation to these duties*'.[75]

These days we are constantly being reminded of our duties as active citizens. '*Citizenship is not a passive activity. It is about making a contribution.*'[76] Government policy at the time of writing, is vigorous in promoting our duties as citizens and is even making citizenship a compulsory part of the school curriculum. At the same time the welfare system is notorious for encouraging a notion of dependence, which is now two generations old. Many people have got used to receiving subsistence levels of support and have neither the energy, nor the inclination, to give back to society. State benefits such as Incapacity Benefit, whilst providing much needed support to individuals and their families, also require people to prove that they are incapable of contributing or are 'economically inactive'.

At the heart of community connecting is the belief that everyone has something to offer. Most of us want to be able to give to as well as to receive from our society. There are different ways to give. We look out for our neighbours; support our favourite charities through volunteering or donating money; lobby to change an unjust law or system; run an event to raise money for a good cause; or simply take part in community activities like cleaning up a local park.

This chapter examines how people with disabilities can expand their networks through the contribution that they make. It looks particularly at:

- campaigning
- volunteering
- exchange
- work
- creating opportunities.

It is evident that in our society people with disabilities are often denied their rights as citizens. They are frequently denied the right to vote and can also be effectively denied access to facilities and services that many other citizens enjoy. What is less obvious is that people with disabilities can also be denied the opportunity to give to the society they live in. Without this opportunity people with disabilities may:

- not have a chance to make a difference in the world
- miss out on valuable routes to meeting people who have a common interest
- miss out on a way of gaining status and confidence in their own eyes and in the eyes of their community.

People with disabilities need to have opportunities to take action and contribute in a way that suits them. Some might be attracted to campaigning work; others may want to volunteer their time; and others may simply want a job.

CAMPAIGNING

Many people with disabilities have had traumatic experiences in the hands of the social care and health systems. They have suffered from lack of support and, in some cases, from abuse. They have often been denied the chance to learn or excel. These experiences lead some people to try to change the system to ensure that others don't suffer as they have. Campaigning groups such as People First, Survivors Speak Out and Age Concern, lobby for individuals across a range of different issues.

Partners in Policymaking is a programme that enables people with disabilities to develop skills in political activity alongside other people with disabilities as well as carers. Through these activities they may develop self-esteem and status. They may also develop strong friendships with like-minded people.

Monica has been involved with People First for several years. Last year she was also a participant on a Partners in Policymaking course. She takes part in People First conferences in Britain and in Europe and has made lots of friends through these. In particular, she visits Petra in Germany and Andrew in Manchester and now has a strong network of more local friends made through Partners in Policymaking who she talks to on the phone and visits from time to time. One of the most important aspects of conferences is talking to people and going out for drinks afterwards. Sometimes they talk about work and sometimes not. Monica finds that through People First and Partners in Policymaking she has met people who have the same values and with whom she has things in common. They often start off talking about issues and then talk about other things outside of work.

She says that being part of campaigning work 'makes you feel that there's someone there' and has helped her stave off depression. People no longer treat her disrespect- fully and Monica has learned how to stand up for herself. She is emphatic that relationships made through this work are very different to those she has made with people who support her.

VOLUNTEERING

Volunteering can be a very valuable experience for people with and without disabilities. Volunteering can offer:

- work experience in an area or field they are thinking of moving in to – to add something to their CV and increase their chances of getting a job
- a taster of something different before taking the plunge and getting a job in that field
- something to do
- an opportunity to meet new people
- an opportunity to give something back to the community
- an increase in knowledge and skills
- a chance to pursue an interest or a dream
- a chance to have fun
- a way of improving an individual's feelings of value and self-worth.

Before individuals take on a voluntary role, it is useful to consider what they wish to gain from it and whether volunteering is an appropriate route to take. And, as always, we need to consider exactly what voluntary activity the individual is interested in and how she might be supported to take part in it. This may mean going through a number of alternatives before finding one that works,

rather than seizing the first opportunity that presents itself. Volunteering needs to be well-organized and all volunteers need to be given recognition for what they do.

When the right place is found it can change an individual's life in a variety of ways. Not only can the person be valued and appreciated in a way that may have never happened before; she may also be given the opportunity to help others.

My name is Muriel. I am sixty years old and I have lived in this house for just over a year. Every Friday morning I go to the local old people's home, where I clean mats, wipe tables and make cups of tea for the residents. I enjoy chatting to one lady who I have known a long time as she lived in the village where I used to stay. I have tea and a biscuit with her. I like helping old people – my Mum is now old and needs people to look after her.

Volunteering can also help people to meet their neighbours and become part of their local community.

Philip attends his local church. A few months ago, the minister was looking for volunteers to serve communion. She asked people to put their hands up at the end of the service and Philip stuck his hand in the air. The minister met with the volunteers to explain what to do and then they got started. Philip enjoys it tremendously. Giving out communion is an important job and it gives Philip a status in the church that he never had before. He is aware of the importance of the role he is performing but isn't overwhelmed by it. People enjoy his nice, informal style.

At the same time, individuals can make friends with people who have a common commitment. For Stan, volunteering opened up a wealth of opportunities.

Everyone I had met told me of the cantankerous elderly man called Stan who had two years ago moved into the large bungalow in a quiet residential area of suburban Bristol. Stan's reputation of being a belligerent, awkward and difficult person to be with preceded him wherever he went.

People would say, "There's just no pleasing Stan, whatever you do for him, he'll just complain. It's a waste of time even trying". There was a sense of exasperation, as if Stan's support workers had tried everything for him, but all they had got in return was criticism and ingratitude. Workers in the day service felt the same way about Stan. Despite all their efforts, they had not found anything for Stan to do that he would stick at for more than a couple of days.

It was clear that Stan had been offered a lot of things to do. It seemed that none of these things were what he really wanted. So what did Stan really want? I realised that no one had yet asked Stan what he truly aspired to or what he really wanted in his life and in the future.

I spent time with Stan, getting to know him, without putting pressure on myself, or him, to try and find a service or an activity that would work immediately. This was very liberating for everyone involved. We mapped out Stan's involvement in his community, his relationships and preferences and thoughts and aspirations for the future.

All of us were taken aback slightly when Stan insisted on focusing on living with Dolly Parton, the country singer and Charlie Dimmock, the gardening presenter. Many people just chuckled at Stan's apparently unreasonable requests for female companionship and said that we should not indulge Stan in his silly fantasy world. But we didn't stop. We took Stan seriously and respected his dreams for the future. As the maps and packs full of photos and artwork grew, so too did Stan's confidence in expressing his vision for the future. We felt that it was important to respect these views and explore the statements further. We explained to Stan that a close relationship with the two celebrities of his dreams was unlikely and then we began to unpick what his vision was really about.

There were three strands to Stan's vision for the future. There were the two female celebrities. Then there were the two things that the women were famous for: Country & Western music and gardening. It was a synthesis of these three strands that proved a key in creating Stan's plan. By talking with Stan over a period of nearly three months, we shaped the detail of his plan into a more achievable form, with a threefold focus: female company, light gardening and Country music. There were no sniggers now from Stan's wider support team and we drew up a three-month action plan.

Stan and one of his support workers volunteered to water some community flowerbeds to help with the efforts towards the annual 'Village in Bloom' competition. They spent an hour over lunchtime each day watering the flowerbeds with a watering can borrowed from the local church, and within a week of being out there on the street watering the flowers they had been approached by scores of neighbours, fellow gardeners and assorted passers by, all keen to chat and interested in the public flower display.

It was here that they met Viv, who was a care assistant at another group home in the area so she vaguely knew both Stan and his support team. While Stan watered the flower display, Viv chatted about what she had been doing over the previous weekend. Viv and her husband, along with a large group of other local enthusiasts, had travelled to Devon for a big Country music event where everyone had dressed up in Wild West clothes and danced the night away. Within a week Stan's support team had approached Viv to see if similar events happened locally.

The rest is history. Line dancing and Country & Western music are not everyone's cup of tea but the people that get involved were a very friendly and welcoming crowd. The first time Stan and I attended the local Country Music Hoe Down was a real eye-opener. People came from miles around to dress up and dance the night away. Stan was bowled over, especially when the woman singing Dolly Parton numbers pecked him on the cheek after the set.

Stan has stopped his watering duties over the winter but when springtime comes I know that the local Community Action Team will contact him to see if he is interested in giving them a hand again. The Country Music event happens locally every month now and every month it becomes more popular. Stan now gets a lift from a friend of Viv's who lives down the street.

Things aren't perfect in Stan's life, but they are very different. Stan says that things are better because now he has got some of the things that he wants.

Although the benefits of volunteering in terms of developing friendships and real purpose in life are obvious, there is a fine line between volunteering and unpaid work. For example, someone volunteering in a business alongside other workers who are all being paid to do the same job is different from someone volunteering alongside other volunteers.

It is likely that some dilemmas will arise in relation to this kind of voluntary activity and time should be taken to think things through.

Linda is a community connector working in the North West of England. She supports people with learning disabilities to build networks. One of the men she works with is called Joey. She describes him as one of the funniest people she has ever met. He has limited communication, attends a day centre five days a week and lives with another man with disabilities. Because he is so immediately likeable, Joey has developed good networks of his own. He is rarely at home and he spends most of his time at his neighbour, Kevin's house – a contact he made himself. Kevin says,

"He's just a fella what just came over and we've never got rid of him since". They go shopping together and Joey enjoys fighting with the kids. When Kevin gets home from work, he often finds Joey sitting at his kitchen table – he gets up and offers Kevin a cup of tea.

Joey is hard-working and cleans all the time. Staff were keen that he had opportunities to get more involved in his local community. Someone suggested that he could develop a relationship with an old person in his community who he could help out by making a cup of tea and clearing up – something that any one of us might do for a neighbour. Most staff members were opposed, feeling that Joey would be taken advantage of. Joey is keen but so far the situation is unresolved.

Ultimately, the decision whether to volunteer or not is a personal choice and the community connector should support the focus person to make the right choice for herself.[77]

EXCHANGE

There are ways in which people can exchange their talents rather than just volunteer them. Local Exchange Trading Systems (LETS) have been set up throughout Britain.[78] '*LETS are local non-profit networks for trading all kinds of goods and services without money*'.[79] Stirling and Alloa LETS scheme has set up a particular service – LETS Make it Better – that supports people with mental health problems to become involved in the trading network. One service-user commented:

I think it is an excellent scheme – it gave me something where I felt I was part of it. I wasn't on the outside looking in with other people doing things. It gave me a reason to get up in the mornings, especially when I was working in the office, and I made friends.

The local psychiatric nurse believes that, '*it is a great opportunity for people with mental health problems to make a positive contribution*'. Recently, a couple of people with learning disabilities have also joined Stirling and Alloa LETS.

The scheme runs a café in a community centre, which is open every day for lunch. People can pay with either groats (LETS currency) or money. Katie started working there every Wednesday a few weeks ago. At the moment she goes with her support worker, who is also a member. Katie earns groats through her work in the café, and she intends to spend them at the trade fair or exchange

them for services from other LETS members. She enjoys it very much and often meets her friend Sheila, who has been involved in LETS for several months. Sheila was introduced to LETS by an occupational therapist at the hospital where she used to live. She and her husband, Pete, are heavily involved in the scheme. As well as working in the café, Sheila organized the bingo night for LETS, which, as she says, was a 'big responsibility'. The scheme has regular social nights to enable members to meet each other, finding that people prefer to trade when they have had a chance to get to know each other a bit. The social nights are open to members and their families and are therefore attended by a wide cross-section of local people.

Sheila says that '*she loves it to bits and has a made a lot of friends*'. She 'spends' the groats she has accumulated at the trade fair in exchange for vegetables, grown by Kevin, another member of the LETS scheme. Pete gardens at the café and may help Kevin out next year with his vegetables.

'*In order to work effectively LETS needs to have as wide a skills base as possible and reflect society as a whole.*'[80] The challenge for any LETS scheme is to involve enough members of the community, and to encourage buoyant trading.

One travelling member of the Stirling and Alloa LETS who has recently moved on said in her farewell letter:

When people from home have asked me about LETS I've said to them, 'Stirling and Alloa LETS is incredible; I just joined and had an instant community; I went from knowing nobody, to having housing, weekly organic vegetables, and a family of supportive friends within a week of joining.'

Of course, exchanging does not have to be done in a formal way, as in a LETS scheme. In our everyday lives, we are exchanging things on a daily basis. Many people with disabilities, however, do not have the opportunity to be a part of this aspect of community, this ebb and flow of exchange and favour.

When Michelle's friends at the swimming pool helped her to fundraise to buy a new van, she was able to offer to do favours for other people in a way that had never before been possible.

She is now able to help other people by giving them lifts to some of her classes. She often collects a friend on the way to the floral art class, for example, and sometimes takes her to the flower market to collect materials for the class too. Michelle has been going to the floral art class for several years. She really enjoys it. It's a very calming activity and Michelle likes the smell of the flowers, the relaxed atmosphere and the friendly people. People bring in greenery and flowers from their own gardens and they are happy to share them with Michelle, who doesn't have any suitable greenery in her own garden. In return, Michelle often buys extra oasis at the flower market so that she can share it with the other flower arrangers at the class, who don't have transport to get to the flower market.

EMPLOYMENT

There are a lot of people with disabilities who simply want a job. A 1996 survey by Glenn and Lyons showed that more than 65 per cent would like a paid job and 45 per cent of that number could be fast-tracked into work with a minimum of support.[81]

However, work for people with disabilities has traditionally been viewed quite differently to work for other people. In the days when people with disabilities were treated as cursed or evil, hard work was seen as a way of driving the devil out. Later, it became used as a punishment for people. Workhouses were set up to enable destitute people, those with disabilities among them, to repay the debt that, it was believed, they owed to society for taking care of them.

Latterly, the work of people with disabilities, such as making postbags, weaving baskets or sticking on labels, has enabled institutions to make money and therefore survive. This kind of piecework or sheltered workshop is still used as a training ground for a real job – but that real job seldom materialises. Such work provides respite both for services and for carers, but most tellingly of all it often provides more jobs for supervisory professionals than it does for people with disabilities themselves.

These kinds of work all focus on grouping people with disabilities together to do the same job, rather than viewing people as individuals with different gifts and capacities. They all disregard the contribution that people with disabilities can make to their communities and their potential to earn real wages doing a real job.

People who need less support have always been more likely to get a job than people with high support needs. During the 1970's, 'supported employment' was developed to offer individual assistance to people wanting to gain employment.

A paid professional took the role of job seeker, supporter or sometimes of job coach.

> As supported employment has evolved, practitioners have recognised that the preferences and personality of the job seeker, the willingness of the workplace culture to accept and adapt to the person, the informal resources and contacts available to the person, and the credibility and style of the support staff are all at least as important as the formal task skills in determining whether someone gets – and more importantly keeps – a job. Employment is now widely accepted as a realistic goal for people with learning difficulties, including those with more significant impairments and higher support needs.[82]

From 1996 to 1999, Kristjana Kristiansen, working at the University of Trondheim in Norway, conducted a research study into employment for people with learning disabilities. The study revealed that income, although important, was not the main benefit for the individuals concerned. Not only did employment extend the networks of many of the people involved, but it also revealed two other significant benefits for people with disabilities and their networks: workers were seen differently and they learned more about life.

Being seen differently

Work changes the quality of existing relationships. The perception of people with disabilities by friends and family is often altered once they have a job. One woman commented, '*People I know see me at work, people remember me there*', implying that that is what they associate her with now.

Erik was the only member of his family in work. His neighbour talked about how he saw Erik differently now that his family depended on him.

A woman whose daughter had a reputation for being challenging, had seen her daughter move out of an institution into her own flat. Overall she had been astonished and delighted by how well her daughter had adapted, but it wasn't until she saw her at the garden centre where she worked that she allowed herself to see her daughter differently: '*That was when she started being an adult in my eyes*'.[83]

In these instances, work had undoubtedly enhanced the quality of existing relationships in the individuals' lives.

Learning about life

For many years service developments for people with disabilities have been based on the 'readiness' model, which assumes that people have to be prepared for the world before they can enter it. People have been taught how to cook, clean and socialise in the artificial environments of an institution where those skills are rarely needed. This strategy has proved both patronising to people with disabilities and ineffective as a way of learning.

Taking a different perspective, the Norwegian study analysed how much one woman could learn from the natural interactions of her colleagues.

Jenny works in a hotel with twelve other women. Every morning they meet up for coffee. On Mondays and Fridays the women discuss their weekend, what they are going to do and what they did. These are Jenny's favourite times.

The other women treat Jenny in the same way as they treat each other. Their views and activities broaden her horizons in ways she really appreciates. From the conversations over coffee she has learned what women think, feel and do. She is living alone for the first time in her life and picks up tips on maintaining a home. They talk about hair and clothes. She went to a colour analyst with them and began to wear green – a colour she had never worn before – and to streak her hair.

Jenny had been in a relationship where her partner had a lot of power over her. She has learnt a lot about relationships from the women's discussions about men and what they will and won't tolerate from their partners.

Jenny has learnt most from watching and participating in discussions with her colleagues. The only thing they are conscious of teaching her is to stand up for herself and make her own decisions. Years of institutional life had left her asking for permission for almost everything she did. Some of the women are politically active and Jenny has now joined the union. Two of the women share her faith and for the first time she has been able to talk about her belief in God with others.

For Jenny, and for other people in the study, the best thing about work was the relationships they developed. One person said that there were '*lots of people (at work) who are nice to me.*' Another woman was depressed that the restaurant where she worked would be shut at Christmas because she would miss the company of her workmates.

The support of co-workers is both typical and natural when people with severe disabilities are in workplaces.[84] Furthermore, studies have shown that people with disabilities often enhance the working lives of their colleagues:

Jill has been instrumental in bringing about positive changes in the lives of her co-workers while working to enrich her own. Through the development of personal relationships at the work place, Jill has succeeded in changing negative perceptions that were held by co-workers regarding persons with disabilities just by allowing them the opportunity to know her and experience her enthusiasm for life. She has recommended holding small gatherings to celebrate co-workers' birthdays, and encouraged management to install coat racks and purchase lab coats to safeguard clothing. The manager of the department describes her as a 'valued member of the team' and further reports that Jill is forever coming up with new ways to improve the work environment'.[85]

However, natural supports are not always available in the workplace but even when they are, turning a colleague into a friend is not always an easy process.

Josh and Will are two young men with learning disabilities who live in a Scottish city. Both have bad reputations and Will requires two-to-one support at all times. Both of them were keen to work and staff began looking for jobs for them. One morning one of their support team, Liz, got talking to one of the security men in their office block. After chatting for a while, Liz asked him if he needed staff at all. He was a bit reluctant at first but Liz assured him that they would provide support at all times and the job would be done. Josh and Will are both working there now one day a week. They love their work so much that Will only needs one-to-one support while he is there. There are four other security guards who work there regularly and they get on well with them. It is still hard for Will to differentiate between staff and workmates. He invited one of his workmates out to the pub one evening and had such a good time that he wanted to do it every night. He was disappointed that it was not possible. Staff members are now looking at how they can support Will to take friendship gradually and make social links outside, as well as within, work.

Some people go out to work specifically because they want to meet people and make friends. For most of us it is more complex than that. We work for a combination of the reasons identified earlier. We value the status work gives us, the money we earn, and the company of colleagues. For us to support

people with disabilities to find a job with the sole aim of developing their relationships, is to limit their potential. Work also needs to provide income, status and independence. However, as the Norwegian study shows, there is no doubt that it can be a very good way to develop networks.

Fiona's story shows how important these networks can be in life:

I was born in 1964. My childhood was much the same as any other person with a learning difficulty. I went to a special school. My parents did not wrap me up in cotton wool and they encouraged me all the way.

In 1980 I left school and started at an Adult Training Centre. In 1988 I started to get fed up with the system at my day centre and moved on to another centre. Here I made friends with a woman who lived in a community house. I applied to the same place and moved there in 1990. About this time I left the day centre to go on a social skills course at college for two years.

In 1992 I finished college and went on a job placement scheme in the hope of getting a job. In January 1993 I started work at a local supermarket.

Two and half years ago I went into a diabetic coma. I was in hospital for three months and off work for six months. I was back at work two months when the supermarket was taken over by another company. The staff remained the same but the way they worked changed and some people left. That was difficult, as they were my friends. They treated me as an equal, remembered my birthday, and I got to go on nights out.

CREATING OPPORTUNITIES TO CONTRIBUTE

When no opportunities in the community exist for the person we are supporting, we can either look wider or take a community development approach and create them ourselves. Duncan Yates describes this process:

There seemed to be very few places in the community where I was working where the people I supported could feel safe to freely express themselves. I thought an inclusive setting was necessary for them to gain confidence and develop their skills and interests.

I knew that the process of including a group of disabled people in a new and often hostile community would not be altogether easy and so I needed to create a process

for which I had an interest and sufficient energy. I had previously worked as a Community Arts worker and had a longstanding personal interest in making things and enabling other people to express themselves through art. Art was my passion and area of interest so art was the vehicle I used.

Weekly groups were held in a range of community buildings in the area. I hired the venues and took along a variety of art materials. I sometimes hired specialist art teachers to facilitate particular sessions. Themes began to emerge. Certain individuals appeared immediately liberated by the chance to have a large space full of creative opportunities. We used music, essential oils, fabrics, paint and plaster. We made enormous wall hangings, sculptures and colour soaked murals.

After a few months I started to look for opportunities in partnership with other agencies. Working alongside the local Council's environmental development department, a team of us replanted an ancient apple orchard. We got our photos in the local paper and in the process introduced ourselves to a good number of local activists and people involved in good works. All of them were interested in developing their community for and all of them were very pleased that we had managed to enhance their neighbourhood with a new orchard at no cost to them at all.

News of the vibrant and popular group spread and soon we were invited to attend the local annual arts festival. We offered to provide a series of workshops for the local people attending the arts festival. In our publicity we made no mention that we were largely a group of people with learning disabilities. There was no need to. We were offering creative opportunities to all local people, without exception. We wanted people of all levels of experience and ability to attend our workshop. The idea was to include everybody. It didn't matter if the workshop participants had not taken part in a specific arts activity since childhood or if they had a degree in ceramics. We welcomed everyone, as everyone had something to offer. Some people brought their mischievous sense of humour or their unstoppable conversation, whilst others took part yet remained happily reflective and quiet. There was room for each approach.

There was a series of design-and-build workshops during the week that culminated in a final daylong festival art workshop where the whole town turned out. At least, that's what it felt like. It was such a thrill to look around and see people of all ages sitting shoulder to shoulder working as fellow artists, equally interested in their piece and making plans for the future together.

It was only a beginning. For some individuals nothing more came of it. For others it was the start of a relationship that was to continue. When we start to connect with people, it leads to more connections, a sense of belonging and inclusion.[86]

ELCAP is an organization working in East Lothian in Scotland. A few years ago it was funded by the Mental Health Foundation to undertake work on community connecting for older people with learning disabilities, the Growing Older with Learning Disabilities programme (GOLD). Lesley, an Area Resource Worker, with the agency, has followed the programme since its inception. It started by asking older people with and without learning disabilities in the area, what they wanted. Their answers were very similar. They wanted tea dancing, social afternoons, gentle exercise, carpet bowling. Although there were clubs running in the area, people didn't seem to know about them or use them very much. So the GOLD programme started by setting up an Accordion Club that was open to everyone. The main problem was that not many community members turned up. Lesley thinks that they thought it was a club just for people with learning disabilities. After eight weeks a local pub decided to take it on, and is still running it. After that the clientele became a lot more mixed and the club makes a valuable contribution to the local music scene.

Having learnt from that experience, the next club set up by the GOLD programme was a tea dance. That has been running now for two years. It was well attended by the community from the first, but initially people found it difficult to mix. Seeing this, Lesley did some work with the staff on how to introduce people and mix. Staff rotas were changed so that the staff members that accompanied the people with learning disabilities were older themselves and often more outgoing. Lesley asked another person at the tea dance who knew what to do to show a member of staff how to dance. In this way barriers were broken down and there is now a lot more mixing. Lesley feels that it would have been a lot quicker if staff had known what they were doing from the beginning, but it was a learning process. Community members have pretty much taken over running the tea dance now. They look out for the members with learning disabilities, and although sometimes they struggle with treating people as equals, they are working hard to change attitudes they have grown up with.

Carpet bowls has also been a great success. This was set up in the leisure centre and has worked from the start. It is fully inclusive and great fun. Members of the local bowling club moved over to join in the winter and have invited the carpet bowls members to social events at the bowling club in the summer.

As a result of the activities set up by the GOLD programme, the older people with learning disabilities are much more widely known and accepted in the local community. The community has benefited from their presence but also from the existence of more activities.

Lesley also runs a volunteer scheme as part of her job. It is there that she has seen examples of deeper friendships. Volunteers are carefully matched and some work very well. One person has been taken in to the heart of a volunteer's family. Another volunteer now defines herself as a friend.

Lesley's approach to her work involved joining the local community council and taking every opportunity to 'develop community for the whole community'. She too is convinced of the need to prioritise community connecting work: '*Many people are living in, but not part of their communities. People need to see the people we support as valuable members of the community*'.

The work of Duncan Yates and the GOLD project are both examples of specific attempts to build 'social capital' in communities for the benefit of all.

In the last three chapters we have examined different strategies that could provide opportunities for connection: community mapping, using networks and making a contribution. In Chapter Three, we outlined ways in which you might choose a strategy. If one doesn't work you can choose another and you may develop ideas of your own on ways forward.

Whatever strategy you adopt you will need to think about how to support relationships once they start to form and how to withdraw without damaging the relationship. We discuss this in the following chapter.

chapter seven
sustaining friendships

Good friendships are fragile things and require as much care as any other fragile and precious thing.

Randolph Bourne

There is an implicit assumption in community connecting work that, at some point in the future, the person in the 'connecting' role will become redundant because the connection will be self-sustaining. This chapter considers one of the most problematic questions involved in community connecting work: 'How do I know when I'm no longer needed?' This is perhaps the least-developed area of community connecting but understandably so, since it only happens after the initial work – that we are still discovering how to do – has been done. Consequently, our reflections are preliminary. We still have much to learn from experience. It does seem, however, that one of the major mistakes we make with community connecting is letting go too soon.

'Creatively connecting people happens over time not over night.'[87]

Occasionally friendships take off and need no extra nurturing, but in most cases some ongoing support is required. Individuals and community members are often inexperienced in developing friendships with each other. People with disabilities may not have had the opportunity to practice phoning people,

asking how they are, exchanging gifts and cards, being concerned for others and all the other natural gestures of friendship. Community members may feel unpractised at relating to people with disabilities as equals. Both sides may need support in understanding and relating to one another for longer than we may have anticipated. Keeping in touch and being sensitive to what is happening in the relationships is key. Backing off completely can leave both parties floundering in the new relationship.

Pat Beeman and George Ducharme describe this as learning to 'walk with' the person. This can be frustrating, but there is no blueprint to follow here. It is just a case of allowing the time and providing the appropriate support for each individual.

Kathryn Mazak, who has been a community builder at Options in Community Living for ten years, talks of the importance of sustaining relationships. She describes her policy as one of being 'relentlessly present' in the same situations with an individual. She tells a story about supporting Pat to join a sea-fishing club. Once an invitation had been issued to the club, Kathryn accompanied Pat but made a deliberate effort not to sit with him. They always went on outings and got lifts with other members of the club. All the time she was revisiting in her mind whether it was the right situation for him. After a while she began to consider how she could get out of the club and allow Pat to fend for himself. The turning point came when she was unable to go on an outing so Pat went without her. The other members began to recognise him as a fisherman in his own right. Kathryn advocates attempting to relax and believe in the competence of the community.

Sometimes it is very difficult to get out of the developing relationship, which becomes three way rather than two way, and a community connector might be stuck going along for several months or even years. Planning for withdrawing needs to start almost immediately the connection is made.

Sometimes the community connector provides not only emotional but practical support that needs to be replaced. Linda, a community connector in the North West of England, is acutely aware of the exiting dilemma. She has introduced John to a wheelchair basketball club and been with him several times. Now that he knows everyone there she plans to withdraw. Initially she will still take him in the car but wait outside. Once he is comfortable she plans to support him to get a taxi on his own.

Transport is again the issue with another individual, Alan, who Linda has supported to join the samba school. It has been a great success and Linda now wants to withdraw. Initially she plans to follow Alan from a distance as he gets the bus. She plans to ask someone from the samba school to meet him at the bus stop and to make sure he gets home safely.

It is important to remember, however, that whilst the community connector or support worker might withdraw from the relationship, they may still be required for other support needs. People who rely on support with personal care, for example, have an ongoing need for this and it is unfair on both the individual and their new friend to expect the friend to undertake personal care.

Not all relationships will develop into friendships, not all memberships of a club will lead to connections outwith that activity. We need to remember that we are only providing opportunities and cannot force the issue. As in all friendships, we may sometimes have to admit that it has not worked and begin searching for an alternative connection. We also need to remember that there are many different levels of friendship and that the only people who can judge the value of a relationship are those directly involved in it.

Things to watch out for:

- there may be a tendency to overload new relationships with lots of demands
- there may be confusion over what a friend is – for example some people may have learned that a friend is someone who will do what you tell them to
- there could be a possibility of rejection – we need to help individuals unde stand that sometimes friendships work out and sometimes they don't
- developing new relationships may bring up difficult experiences from the past and we may need to seek extra support in the form of counselling or therapy to help individuals come to terms with these
- there is always the possibility of abuse and we need to reassess risk regularly and look out for the signs of it, without cosseting or overprotecting.

WHAT CAN A COMMUNITY CONNECTOR DO TO SUPPORT FRIENDSHIPS?

The following are signposts to issues that might arise in the development of friendships between people with disabilities, to whom friendship is a new experience, and community members, who are experiencing a different kind of friendship. They will not arise in every case. It need not be the community

connector who supports the relationship, this role could be taken on by another friend, family member or member of the support team.

- Reciprocity – relationships always need to benefit both parties to some extent. What that actually involves is different in every relationship and can only be judged by the individuals concerned – what community connectors can do is to stress the need for it, look for signs of it and, sometimes, support individuals to appreciate each other. Community connectors need to keep seeking ways to promote the person, and their gifts and capacities. Power imbalances may always be present but they need to be open for discussion.
- Modelling – friendships seem easy to us because we have grown up with them. For individuals who have never had experience of friendship the unwritten rules may seem impenetrable. They may need support with practical aspects of friendship, like phoning their friend or writing a birthday card. They may need support with the emotional aspects of friendships, like how to make up when you have had a row, what to do when you feel let down. Individuals can learn by being given an insight into how other friendships work.
- Encouraging – there is a tendency to leave things alone when they are going well, but we need to keep encouraging and solving problems with people. The balance between interfering and supporting is hard to strike but can be done by working in partnership with people.
- Ask: 'Are we there yet?' – Community connectors need to be able to acknowledge when they have done what they can. They need to judge when they can finally let go and allow the relationship to take its natural course.

Throughout the book we have shared ideas, strategies, and stories about developing and supporting friendships and making a contribution to the community. This, and how to support relationships over time, require significant changes within organizations. The final chapter examines these issues.

chapter eight
reflections for organizations

This chapter examines how the practice of community connecting impacts on organizations. It analyses some of the inherent challenges in this work and looks at some strategies for dealing with them, considering in turn the impact on front-line staff, managers, and organizations as a whole. It ends with a word of caution about the potential for the colonisation of community connecting by organizations.

We particularly focus on:

- the role of the organization
- new roles for staff
- implications for managers
- challenges for organizations
- strategies for organizations
- evaluation

THE ROLE OF THE ORGANIZATION

Community connecting is not the sole responsibility of support agencies. It requires commitment from the individual, their family and friends, communities of interest and geographical communities. Yet often it is an organization that needs to support the individual to make the first move.

Person centred planning and community connecting present several challenges to organizations set up to support people, the first of which is accepting the importance of working in a new way. As we have seen, person centred planning and working leads to new kinds of relationships with people – a prioritisation of social as well as clinical needs and a partnership between the individual, their support staff, and their family and friends in planning the future. This inevitably results in a redistribution of power.

For organizations it may mean that services need to be rearranged around an individual rather than a group of individuals. It may mean that staff will be working on their own with a person in new and challenging situations.

If an organization is already working in a person centred way then community connecting is a natural progression. Many people will identify their need for community and relationships, and organizations will have to be committed to supporting these aspects of an individual's plan.

How human service organizations can get in the way

John McKnight has been researching, and working on community connecting for over fifteen years. Noting the ability of human services to distance the community:

> One wonders how it is possible, in a small town of 5,000 people, to find a typical house and have five residents live there for ten years without any effective community relationships. Yet human service systems designed to provide what are called 'community services' often have managed to do just that. [88]

He describes four ways in which human services act as a barrier between individuals and their communities:

1. It is well known that traditional human services focus on what people cannot do rather than exploring their capabilities. This emphasis provides a need for special services designed to fix the deficiency without highlighting the capacity. The individual is denied the opportunity to find their gifts and is therefore unable to contribute to community.

2. Fundamentally, money going to human services is not money going directly to individuals (although the direct payments legislation may go some way towards changing this).

3. Professionals usurp the natural role of people. Human service professionals with special expertise, techniques and technology push out the problem-solving knowledge and action of friend, neighbour, citizen and association. Many local people come to believe that the service way is the only way, and that their task as good citizens is to pay taxes and support charities to provide more services.

4. Surrounding people with services creates a vicious circle. People become institutionalised and dependent. They act in ways that are considered inappropriate. Their actions are taken as evidence for an increase in the services that support them. This distances them still further from the community.

John Lord and Alison Pedlar conducted a study of the effects of human services on the quality of life of 18 people moved out of an institution and into the community in Canada:

> Four years after moving, eight people have only one person apart from paid staff in their social network; the other ten people have two or three people in the their social network. Typically these network members are family or former staff: family members, usually parents, remain people's most frequent contacts and five people have a friend among present or former staff members. One person knows a community member who was recruited to befriend him; one person's sister has actively included him in her network of activities and relationships; and one person is an active member of her church. People's most common roles outside their group homes and day programs are those of consumer and spectator: two or three times a week they visit restaurants and shops or movie theatres or bowling lanes, usually as one among a group of people with disabilities.[89]

This situation is replicated in group-homes and supported-living arrangements across Britain. Many organizations are now recognising the part they have played in distancing individuals from communities and have begun to focus, instead, on gifts. They are also trying to accommodate direct payments and attempting to make room both for community and for family and friends. This way of working not only produces a new role for staff members but also has implications for managers and, in turn, organizations as a whole, especially in the key areas of service design, finance, and risk assessment.

NEW ROLES FOR SUPPORT STAFF

The role of community connecting may well be a new one for workers. It is challenging because there is little precedent for this kind of work, although there are basic lessons we can begin to learn from what others have done. Also, it is

different in every case depending on individuals' desires for their future, on the existing networks they have, and on the opportunities available.

> Addressing this need (for community building) does not have to mean just one more thing for an agency or service provider to be doing or be required to do. Rather, addressing this need does mean doing things differently than they are being done. It does mean a different, rather than an additional role for staff. [90]

Community connecting requires staff to work in new ways. For some people building community is as natural as breathing. Most staff will find it more of a challenge. They will be required to work directly with an individual on a one-to-one basis much of the time. For those used to work in institutional settings this may initially be isolating. They will need to be able to see the gifts in a person and, where they are not obvious, tell other people about them. They will need to be able to speak to strangers and ask things of them. They may find their own boundaries threatened as their relationship with the person they support becomes deeper. They will need to be able to work out solutions to difficult situations and consider risk in a new way. Most importantly of all they will need conviction both in the individual they are supporting and in the community at large. And they will need to have resilience – to try again ... the twentieth time.

It is important that staff members undertaking the role of community connector are supported to build on their existing skills, as well as to develop new ones. Although this is a new role, it draws heavily on the core interpersonal skills of any good support worker.

One of the most challenging aspects of the work is that it raises questions that we have not had to face before; questions about professional and personal boundaries; questions about beliefs and attitudes and questions about the nature and quality of the relationship we have with the individual that we support. These questions coalesce in five key areas.

Intimacy

Community connecting requires people to share their dreams with us. We may be used to helping with intimate bodily tasks, but being trusted with a person's dreams is a new level of intimacy. It is a privilege and a responsibility:

'Tread softly because you tread upon my dreams.'[91]

Workers may find that they share more of themselves with the focus person and this may initially feel uncomfortable. One service-user described telling his keyworker, when starting to look at opportunities to make connections, about his desire to go to the football. His keyworker told him that his brother worked at the local football club. Although the service-user had known that member of staff for seven years, he had never even been aware that his keyworker had a brother, let alone that he was interested in football.

We need to be aware of any discomfort within ourselves and find ways of talking it over with the focus person, other members of our team or with our manager.

Creativity

Community connecting is hard work. It requires creative thinking on many different levels, to find new ways of overcoming obstacles, or working round them. It requires asking for help from other people and challenging the precon-ceptions that many people frequently have. Because of this, it is rewarding but exhausting.

Bravery

It doesn't take much courage to go the pub with someone to share a drink and a chat. It takes a lot more courage to go to the pub, look out for people that the individual might get on with, engage them in conversation and support the individual to be included in the conversation. Some people, who are natural born community connectors, do this without thinking but most of us struggle with it. However, it is a skill that can be learned, and as it is learned it increas-ingly becomes a key part of the job. It is not necessary to become an extrovert overnight, but it is necessary to learn the skills of asking, engaging, connecting and including.

> The only way to discover if someone would be willing to meet someone or do something with someone is to ask. Sometimes we're reluctant to ask others to do things. We typically expect that people will say 'no'. However, over and over again in the Friends project, staff were amazed at what happened when they simply asked. They thought others would be reluctant or need more information. Over and over again, people simply said 'yes'. And not only 'yes', but 'yes, no problem' or 'yes, have her come over today'.[92]

Confidence

Community connecting requires confidence, in ourselves as people able to connect, in the individual as someone with whom others will want to connect with, and in the community as a reservoir of hospitality.[93]

Willingness to take risks

Community connecting requires a willingness to take risks, on our own behalf and on behalf of the people we support. It also requires us to assess risk carefully and thoroughly and to be able to demonstrate both that we have done so and that we have tried to minimize risk as much as possible.

Most importantly the new role of community connector requires an ongoing and committed belief in the individual and the community in the face of all kinds of adversity. In order to do this, the community connector must make sure that she has adequate support systems including:

- time to unwind
- structured-reflection and problem-solving time with others doing the same work
- good support and supervision from a manager who understands the nature of the work
- time to celebrate success
- a way to measure and evaluate success or failure.

IMPLICATIONS FOR MANAGERS

To run individualised, person centred services you need to manage things you can't control, work with fuzzy boundaries, keep on the edge of the possible.[94]

Supporting staff members in the role of community connector is a great challenge for a manager. By definition, person centred working and community connecting are tailored to the individual, therefore every member of staff will be undertaking a slightly, or perhaps very, different job. The task of the manager is to provide the kind of support and supervision to staff that nurtures learning, encourages creativity and offers a structure for risk-taking. If these core conditions are well established, they will provide a robust back-up to those people at the front line of the work, whatever the specific endeavour they are undertaking.

Managers will face challenges in several key areas:

Time management

Many support agencies operate complicated shift and rota systems that may hinder community connecting efforts. For example, community connecting will

probably require a member of staff to work with a person at the same time every week if they are going to access a particular activity. The manager will need to anticipate this and find ways round it or build it in to the rota.

In order for community connecting work to take root, it needs a significant investment of time from staff. With many other competing demands on staff time, this often seems impossible to achieve. The manager will need to allocate dedicated time for this work and make sure that that time is protected. This may mean that work priorities need to shift and this, in turn, will need to be clearly stated to the whole team, and not just the staff taking on community connecting roles.

How to measure success

In order to encourage ongoing learning, the manager will need to support staff to celebrate success and also to learn from mistakes. The established indicators for measuring success may have little relevance when applied to community connecting work, so new criteria may be needed, and these may well be different for each individual. The manager will need to work closely with individual members of staff to work out the best ways to evaluate individual pieces of work. It will then be the manager's job to support learning in relation to the implications of any evaluation:

- for the individual
- for the individual member of staff
- for the project or organization.

(See the section later in this chapter for more discussion of evaluation.)[95]

Risk

Carson suggests that one of the key tasks facing the manager is to provide front-line workers with '*a framework for making their decisions which promises to support those who follow their policies, even if harm results*'.[96]

Risk in relation to organizations is discussed later in this chapter and we have already seen that it will be a key consideration in this work. What the manager will need to do is offer staff a robust system for evaluating risk and a security that there will be support for decisions taken even if the worst case scenario actually happens.

Training

The decision about who will receive training will probably be in the hands of the manager. Some staff will be obvious candidates for this kind of work. Others will need more encouragement or nurturing. In addition, the manager will need to decide whether she, as manager, needs to undergo training in community connecting in order to support staff in this new role.

It is often necessary to make pragmatic decisions about training since it is costly in terms of time and finance. Managers will need to think carefully about which staff members need to receive a particular type of training. As we have already seen, community connecting work requires inexhaustible energy, commitment and motivation. If one member of staff is undertaking the work alone, this may quickly wane. It is not usually sufficient to have a vanguard of community connectors and no back-up. Managers need to assess energy levels and make sure that there is a second wave to pick-up if these begin to drop.

Team Work

When faced with new challenges and new ways of working, a team will need opportunities to come together and discuss, air views, share problems and stories of success, and cultivate learning. Structured time should be built in for this.

A shift in culture towards seeing service-users in terms of their gifts and contributions can be reflected across the team. Changing the language and focusing on individual staff gifts, skills and interests might be a way into helping a team think about community connecting. In turn, the manager can begin to introduce this language into support and supervision.

Over time, staff will begin to see themselves as teams working around a person rather than a team working for an organization. Having space to reflect on the change towards being a person centred team will be important. A process for developing person centred teams, helps team members to reflect on *their* gifts, strengths, support needs and contributions in the focus person's life.[97]

CHALLENGES FOR ORGANIZATIONS
Service design

As with person centred planning, group living is likely to be a barrier to building community connections:

> Service-mediated groupings present an enormous barrier to community connection – both because people are seen as one of a group of 'people like that', and because people are seen as 'in the care of' someone else – not part of the street, but part of the welfare state. And in practice group living and congregate day services lead all too often to group outings – visits to the community, not connections with it.[98]

Agencies that successfully support people in connecting with their communities are agencies that work with people as individuals. This means supporting them to live in a home of their choice with people of their choice. It means planning their week with them to suit them. For many organizations this means redesigning the services they offer.

Finance

Redesigning services has enormous financial implications in the short term, although it may not prove more expensive in the long term. Support agencies for people with disabilities are finding their budgets squeezed more and more tightly and, in an age of competitive tendering, there is always someone else willing to provide what looks like the same service more cheaply.

Redesigning services is complicated in such a climate, but community connecting is threatened for other reasons too. Firstly it is often seen by agencies as an optional extra; the icing on the cake once the serious business of meeting clinical needs has been attended to. Community connectors across the board testify to a refusal from both purchasers and providers to recognise the importance of their work, which leads to a lack of investment. Agencies need to take seriously the assertion by Jeff and Cindy Strully that *'friendship is a matter of life and death for our daughter'*.[99]

Secondly, low wages for support assistants combined with a buoyant economy result in a high turnover of staff. It is often the case that individuals have barely got to know their new staff member before that member of staff is off again. Trust between an individual and their support team is essential in person centred planning and community connecting work and these relationships take time. Workers need time to build up commitment to the focus person in order to harness their imagination and enthusiasm for this kind of work. Fragmented support leads to a lack of opportunities for people to be introduced into community and therefore has serious implications for the quality of life of service-users.

Any change requires investment in the short term and community connecting work is no exception. It is work, however, that will lead to long-term improvements for individuals, bringing a reduction in the amount of support they need and cutting down their use of services.

At the same time agencies need to remember that community connecting should never be undertaken with the aim of substituting necessary paid support with volunteers:

> Inclusion among the recognised members of a community cannot substitute for public investment in a variety of supports and opportunities for people with substantial, continuing need for assistance. Social support is not a substitute for well-designed services; social support is the foundation for any effective service.[100]

Risk

Community connecting requires organizations to take the risk of believing in community and of trusting those who are unpaid and unaccountable. Most of the time this works out very well, or at least does no harm. But it should be acknowledged that there will be occasions when individuals and community members are vulnerable to exploitation, abuse, and harassment. For community connecting to work these occasions need to be faced. Organizations need to promote a culture where taking risks is acceptable and indeed encouraged, while at the same time ensuring that this risk is managed as much as is humanly possible. This requires courage in a society that is becoming more risk averse and where the concept of community care is already deemed a failure.

To be responsible, organizations need to provide staff and individuals with appropriate ways of assessing and minimizing risk to ensure that both the individuals they support and the community is adequately protected.

For community connecting to be successful, staff members need to be trusted to use their judgement. Organizations need to take the risk of believing in the capability of front-line staff to make their own decisions. Without this, creativity is stifled.

Most importantly of all, organizations need to be seen to back their staff if a well-considered risk doesn't work out. In many organizations staff do not take risks because they do not believe that they are supported to do so.

STRATEGIES FOR ORGANIZATIONS

In researching this book we have found organizations across the UK that have worked out different strategies for community connecting. These include:

- making it integral from the start
- employing a community connector
- accessing a community connector through another agency
- staff development
- working more effectively with family and friends.

Making it integral from the start

The following are examples of four very different kinds of services that have made community connecting integral to their work.

ELCAP (East Lothian Care & Accommodation Project)

The closure of the long stay hospitals and the introduction of the competitive tendering process led to a proliferation of new organizations supporting people with disabilities. Some of these new organizations were set up along traditional lines, providing group homes and day programmes. But a significant number set out to be different, to work with each person as an individual, to tailor support and to make serious efforts to connect with the community.

ELCAP, based in a semi-rural area of Scotland, is in some ways a hybrid. It was set up ten years ago, and although it runs some group services, it put community connecting right at the heart of its service from the start. Linda, the director, acknowledges that it is this part of the service, which feels most vulnerable. Many purchasers don't recognise the value of community connecting, and would find time costed-in for it an easy thing to cut. Much of the time allocated to it needs therefore to be hidden in other costs. ELCAP has created two locality based 'community connector' posts. Although some of what they do can be written into contracts, the majority of their salaries have to be paid through fund-raising.

ELCAP have had significant success in building bridges in local communities. Every attempt was made to move people out of hospital and back into the town where they had originated from sometimes up to forty years earlier. A strong feeling of 'looking after our own' became apparent in the community when some 'incomers' attempted to block ELCAP from purchasing houses in their street. Local people

informed the incomers that the people supported by ELCAP had more right to live in the street than they did.

Where opportunities have not been available in the local community ELCAP staff have started up new initiatives for the benefit of the whole community. A keep fit club started by ELCAP is now run by the local community and afternoon tea dances have proved more popular with locals than with ELCAP users. Linda judged it a success when a member of the local community phoned her up to complain about the attitude of a member of staff towards the person he was supporting. The matter was resolved and Linda was reassured not only by the fact that the community member knew what the attitude should have been but also that she had gone out of her way to advocate for the service user by letting Linda know.

The 'community connectors' are employed because it is difficult for support staff to initiate and develop activities themselves. It may be that they do not possess the necessary knowledge and skills but, even so, shared-services staffing arrangements are often not flexible enough to allow support staff the opportunity to consistently spend their time this way.

Ideally, community connecting should be done by support staff, thereby ensuring that it is available to all those being supported. This would cut across any notion that such work is the preserve of a select few, or that it is somehow separate from the core activity of support. It would also correct any belief that it is easy work compared with traditional support work and would illustrate how much time and effort it can take to build connections.

As with other agencies, recruitment and retention of staff is a big issue. ELCAP is not able to pay support assistants as much as they could earn working at the checkout in the local supermarket.

Ultimately, however, there is a need to plan for sustainability, and where possible for paid support to fade and unpaid support to take over.

Linda feels that some purchasers are insecure about allowing the organization to take risks. One service-user, who has epilepsy, wanted to live on her own. ELCAP joined forces with her care manager to work out an acceptable package and advocate for it with social work managers. Being forced to think about the worst-case scenario all the time colours the thinking and confidence of staff. Linda is clear that it is the organization, rather than individual staff, that takes responsibility for risk, particularly if it doesn't work out.

ELCAP has adopted quite an original strategy to minimize the risk in making local connections. When first set up it asked staff and board members to look out for key people who were well connected in each locality in which they operated. These people now act both as a reference point, and as a community connector when necessary. This kind of local network means that new people can often be informally checked out, minimising the risk right from the start.

ELCAP is clear that community connecting is integral to the service it provides. Although it is not easy to prioritise it, Linda feels that without community connecting the service would be 'two dimensional'.

LEAF

Life, Employment And Friends was set up with the aim of filling the gaps in the lives of many people with support needs. Over the past year it has supported four individuals into paid employment and found seven individuals voluntary jobs. It has set up circles of support for four other people and supported a further six to take up new activities. Kay Mills, the director, is the only paid work-er. She works through a combination of direct practice and mentoring staff to take on community building or facilitating circles themselves.

Kay maintains that the dedicated time she can give to community connecting makes a huge difference to the outcome of the work. She is by nature a very talented community connector. She has lived in the same community all her life, she is genuinely interested in people, and is a difficult woman to refuse. She acknowledges that staff don't find the work easy. Her explanation for this is that:

- *normally it is difficult for them to concentrate on one individual*
- *there is still a strong focus in most support services on meeting basic needs and keeping people safe*
- *risk taking is difficult in registered accommodation*
- *it depends on whether the care manager values the work or not*
- *some staff find it hard to introduce people into new situations*
- *there are some barriers in the community and in families.*

Despite great stories of success, Kay has found it difficult to convince purchasers of the value of the work. She finds that some providers expect staff to do it anyway without any support or training.

Kay works from a strong values base, believing in the individual and in the capacity of the community to include them 'you have to see it for yourself and help others see it'. For those she supports she is looking for loyalty, commitment and someone to be there for them. She knows that there needs to be some kind of reciprocity – that it needs to be fun, or a challenge.

Streets Ahead

Stirling Council has embarked on a programme to close their day centres. A new service, Streets Ahead, has been set up to support people with support needs in community. So far the service is supporting 18 people in voluntary work and mainstream activities. Even after a few months, the manager, Mhairi McAughtrie, knows that families are seeing the difference. People have a lot more to talk about now, and one carer said that she has got her life back as her brother receives support when it suits him – and that includes evenings and weekends. For other carers it is more of a struggle as they were used to the regular hours provided by the day centre.

The service users have been engaged in a variety of activities based on person centred planning. One person bakes for the LETS café. Mhairi plans to offer to extend the opening hours to give users a chance to work in exchange for groats, while offering a longer service to the community. Other people undertake different kinds of voluntary work. One person works for a delivery service for one day a week. He no longer needs a support worker with him that day. Another works in a different café where his colleagues provide him with on-the-job support. Streets Ahead is always at the end of phone but encourages support from other community members wherever possible. Mhairi feels that people are already becoming much better known in their community.

The service has a real advantage in being part of the council. It links with other council services like education and leisure which are now consciously making their mainstream facilities more accessible to people with support needs.

Inclusion Alliance[101]

The mission of Inclusion Alliance is:

'To enable people who need long-term support to lead the lives they, and the people closest to them, choose, as active participants in their local communities.'

Inclusion Alliance is an organization of people with learning difficulties, parents, carers and professionals who work together to include people with learning

difficulties in everyday life. The organization is a response to the desire of people with learning difficulties to lead valued lives that are not segregated from the rest of their fellow citizens. The history of the organization is rooted in campaigning organizations led by parents and service users.

Inclusion Alliance is a not-for-profit organization with charitable status and receives all of its core funding from the City of Edinburgh Council Social Work Department. The Board of Management is user-led and Circles of Support are used as a decision-making process on an individual level.

Inclusion Alliance has made an explicit commitment to a guiding philosophy, namely the values of inclusion and person centred-ness, the Five Accomplishments and the principles of community connecting.

One-to-one support is provided to 13 men and women with learning difficulties and high support needs to lead full lives as members of their local communities. This support is given for 31 hours a week and can be used flexibly according to individual needs and wishes. Currently, most people choose to use the time during the day as an alternative to traditional day centres.

All of the service users have their own one-to-one worker (known as the 'facilitator'), whom they and people close to them have been involved in recruiting. The close relationships that have developed between facilitators and service-users have been crucial in the process of ensuring that the individuals can exercise real choice and control in their own lives.

The individuals use their support time differently. Some use it to access community education and college classes; some for support in work placements or real jobs, and some to participate in leisure and sports activities. Wherever possible, people use community facilities where there are opportunities to spend time and build connections with other members of the community.

The organization strives to encourage a learning culture, where discussion is encouraged, and to spend time reflecting on its progress. These are some of the things the organization is learning:

- *Supporting people to access mainstream community places and activities for six hours a day and five days a week takes effort and planning. What helps is knowing the detail of what works or does not work for each person, and being creative. Also, recognising that a fulfilling life evolves over time.*

- *Transport for people who use a wheelchair is expensive and not always flexible … Transport is an important issue to think about when planning and implementing an individual service that relies on existing public resource, that are not accessible to some individuals.*
- *Maintaining reliable relief cover is the main operational difficulty facing the service … Employing a permanent male and female relief worker would be something to consider in designing and costing a similar project.*
- *Staff members are working on their own for much of the time rather than as part of a team. This requires people that feel comfortable working with a high degree of autonomy and trust. Staff need to be highly motivated and able to 'self-supervise' for much of the time; they require a personal commitment to the individual they support and an ability to really listen to what the person is saying and to respond to them.*

Over time, the organization has watched many connections being made between service-users and other community members as people take part in community activities. When asked what they thought of the service, parents and carers, as well as service-users said:

- *"He's more relaxed and comfortable when new people are around."*
- *"People are able to go at their own pace – no pressure."*
- *"People are making connections they would not otherwise have made."*
- *"He was a very withdrawn, unsociable, uncommunicative, anxious young person who has blossomed into a confident, outgoing, talkative person willing to try new and varied activities."*
- *"I've got friends."*

Employing a community connector

Person centred planning and community connecting are not integral to the set up of many established organizations. A common strategy for an organization beginning to prioritise community connecting is to employ a community connector.

Options in Community Living in Madison pioneered this model. Kathryn Mazak worked as a community connector there for ten years and some of the lessons she learnt there have already been referred to in this book (see Chapter Seven). In *Members of Each Other*, John and Connie Lyle O'Brien attribute Options in Community Living's success in community connecting to a number of things: the good quality of daily support that people receive; Kathryn Mazak's skill as a community connector; the use of an experienced consultant to the organization; and budgetary flexibility to create the position of community connector.

Community connectors are normally employed to:

- kick-start initiatives that other staff do not have time to implement
- mentor support staff in community connecting.

Community connectors have adopted different ways of going about their task.

The community development model

Jill works in a Scottish city for a large voluntary organization. She is responsible for building community for ten people who have recently moved out of hospital. Jill has a background in community development and so began with a strong sense of community and what it is. Her strategy was to find the information first then store it until it was time to use it. She jokes that she is always working in some way, adopting Tom Kohler's strategy of 'always lurking, swimming quietly through the shoals of citizens'.

She spent her first few months in post in the community: walking about, talking to the 'movers and shakers', spending time in the community centres, getting in touch with the local newspaper and investigating any partnerships working in the area. She found the 'third place' – a local community centre but acknowledges that 'it is about identifying people, not just places. I do the rounds, have a natter'. She sees her role as awareness raising in the community and changing attitudes, being always accessible and always available.

Jill says she is lucky in that she works in an area where there is already a strong community spirit and that 'people have been brilliant'. She has spent time talking to the community forum, where local businesses, voluntary organizations, churches and people meet, explaining her role. She and the service users have taken stalls at community events. Jill says that you have to be prepared for the 'long sit'. It is only now, a year into her job that things are really beginning to come together.

Jill believes that some people, who have been institutionalised for a long time, need support to get back into community. She set up a 'bridging class' with the

Adult Learning Project for four people who used her service and wanted to sing. The four-week course was a great success and now two of the individuals are happy to take part in a mainstream class. One has dropped out completely and the other wants to go on to another 'bridging class'. Another woman Jill supports, Ellen, has been baking for the community centre for the last few months. Jill has a good contact in Shirley, the woman who runs the community centre. She intends to approach her to see if Ellen can come in and work in the café selling the cakes she has made.

For Jill, being in community is about taking risks. Although she tries to do the groundwork she works a lot on gut-feeling. She also sees the potential of community building to lessen risk. One service user bought a motorbike. Jill encouraged him to enrol in the local maintenance classes so that he could meet others with the same interest and learn from them.

Jill also works with staff. She feels that they could be more creative about the support they offer to people. Some staff members are beginning to be more adventurous but others see it as a luxury only to be indulged when there is nothing more important to be done. Jill feels strongly that community connecting is what staff should be doing and that more time should be given to it otherwise 'you can take people out and hold them hostage in their home'.

One person at a time

Linda was employed for a year to develop Circles of Support by a social services department in the North West of England. She works with eight people, all of whom were referred by the managers of their day services. Linda identifies this as a problem, saying that it would be much better had the individuals concerned chosen the service rather than been chosen for it as some of them are not interested in developing a circle. She also found working for social services a barrier for some people *'because they automatically think, "OK, what does this person want from me? Do they want long-term commitment? Do they want this person to come and live with me?"'*

Linda started with the person and worked outwards from their interests. Working across communities it wasn't possible for her to take a locality-based community development approach.

Colin wanted to meet more people in his community and was very interested in football. Linda started by taking him down to the local community centre where

they ran a line dancing night. Colin wasn't that interested in line dancing but he liked the folk at the community centre and got on particularly well with the manageress. She suggested in jest that he got a job there. Linda followed it up through the town hall and now Colin does voluntary work on Thursdays. It makes him 'feel really part of it'. Recently Colin moved flats and the manageress and Terry, another friend from the community centre, helped him move and organize a birthday party for his flatmate. '*So he's really developed a friendship there and you know it might only be two people but that's two people he didn't know six months ago*'.

John has made a connection with a wheelchair basketball team, which Linda also joined. She says that she doesn't see circles as just about making friends with able bodied people: '*he's making some good friends there with people who are able bodied and disabled as well*'.

'*I did some work with trying to get Alan to move on from the day service and it was just to no avail – he wasn't interested. We tried college, and we tried several working establishments and I've even supported him to go to work and stuff and its just not what he wants. He wants to be able to go to the day centre when he feels like it. But one of the main things Alan was interested in was drumming. He's a very good drummer.*'

Linda had a contact in the performing arts section of the council and he suggested the local samba school. Alan has been going weekly for the last few months and even dropped his regular Monday club because it clashed. He has been in playing in a club with them. '*He's never been in a nightclub in his whole entire life … he's just brilliant. He just really took to it … I was saying, well on you go and have a wander round and when you are ready come back. I warned him not to take any drugs and not to go out the door without telling me and not to go off with any strange women. I gave him my mobile number … But I was sitting there and he went missing for about an hour. I was a bit worried now so I went looking for him and there he was round the corner with one of the girls from the samba school sitting on his knee.*'

Kenny has been the one person Linda has made no progress with at all yet. She thinks he was referred to her because the day centre found his behaviour so difficult and wanted to get him out. Although she has tried lots of different approaches and activities, she hasn't found anything that really interests him yet.

Linda mentors a lot of staff as part of her work and has found two enthusiastic members of staff, who she hopes will take over with two individuals as she withdraws.

But although she has experienced significant success she has also come across barriers that have made the work demoralising at times. Staff attitudes have impeded the work with certain individuals. And she thinks that expectations placed upon her are exceedingly high. In some ways Linda achieved the results she did because of the work she put in. As well as her 37 hours she went to church with Barry on Sundays, to samba school with Alan on Monday evenings, line dancing with Colin on Fridays and basketball with John on Wednesdays. Now she is ready to 'sit back a bit'.

Although both Linda and Jill's work show how effective community connectors can be, they cannot change the culture of an organization single-handedly. The disadvantage of the model, something that they have both identified, is that it allows core staff to leave community connecting to the community connector, preventing them from seeing it as integral to their own work. And one community connector is unlikely to make a difference to the lives of more than a few people.

Community connectors can be excellent at kick-starting a process of change and mentoring staff, but for organizations to be really effective at community connecting they need to address issues of service change and staff development.

Access a community connector from another agency

It is sometimes possible to access the services of a community connector who is employed independently by an outside (usually voluntary) agency to work specifically with people in relation to community connecting.

The benefits of having someone independent of the support provider are:

- The individual does not need to be linked to any other service in order to access the community connector. Often the most isolated people are those who don't receive any formal services at all and yet community connecting is often an add-on to other services. External community connectors can, in theory, reach those people who are most isolated.
- Because the community connector is not tied to any service, she can be more explicitly accountable to individuals themselves and not the provider agency.

However, the difficulties inherent in this model tend to outweigh these benefits, making it fairly uncommon. Some of the difficulties are:

- The community connector will often need to rely heavily on the back-up support of other staff from residential or day care centres to follow through ideas. This is not always easy since different agencies work to different philosophies, staff ratios and resources.
- There is no ongoing role for the community connector in the individual's life. The relationship is purely developed for the purposes of community connecting. This means that if the connecting strategy doesn't work out, the individual could be left feeling disappointed, or, worse, a failure having invested in another relationship that hasn't worked out.

For these reasons, clarity of purpose and role is even more important for workers taking on the role of external community connector.

Staff development

As we have seen, to be successful community connecting cannot be left up to just one or two individuals within an organization. It is a practice that needs to be embraced by every member of staff. New organizations employing new staff in different roles have found the transition less difficult than existing organizations where jobs are changing and the same people are asked to do different things.

Amado and colleagues worked with six residential services on the Friends Project.

> Its purpose was to learn about and develop methods for the staff of residential service agencies to support people with disabilities in establishing friendships and relationships with non-disabled people in their communities, and to assist people with disabilities in being more part of their communities.[102]

They found that *'the success of this work will depend on staff perspectives toward three things: the individuals with disabilities, community members and the importance of this work.'*[103]

Staff need to be able to:

- believe in community
- map opportunities in the local community
- get to know the person and believe in their gifts

- introduce the person to new places and people
- support the person in new situations and with new relationships
- withdraw when the time is right.

Many of these skills are ones that we use in our own lives every day. The change is in thinking about those skills in relation to work.

Staff can be trained to undertake community connecting with people. They can learn the skills outlined above and those who personally feel quite comfortable in new situations will perhaps find practising them easier than others.

Training is not an end in itself. Staff members will continue to have support needs in relation to this work. They will need to be continuously supported to:

- monitor and evaluate risk
- think of new strategies
- keep motivated when things don't work out
- challenge their own comfort zone
- monitor and evaluate success.

Training must be linked to ongoing peer group support and time must be protected to ensure that this can be prioritised.

A common reaction by staff when faced with the prospect of community connecting work is, 'Oh no, not another thing'. Staff in human services are over-burdened as it is. There is no getting away from the fact that starting to build community means a further investment of time. It takes time to get to know an individual, it takes time to get to know community. But in the long term we are looking to a future where the individuals we support spend more time with friends and less with paid support staff. This does not mean there will be no need for paid support staff, only that people with support needs will be less dependent on them in all aspects of their lives.

Amado has pointed out that community connecting does not necessarily mean doing more, but doing differently.[104] An administrator of one agency in the Friends Project said, '*I used to think that community integration meant doing activities in the community; now I know that it means helping people have friends*'. Instead of going to the café to have lunch with an individual, it means going to the local cafe to meet the locals. It just takes a bit more thought to plan to do something at a regular time each week.

Many staff find this work stretching but richly rewarding. Organizations that invest in training and support their staff to undertake new, challenging, and more autonomous work will find that their retention rates go up. After all, most staff are not in this field of work just for the money.

Ark Housing Association, an agency providing housing and support to people with learning difficulties across Scotland decided to invest in a large-scale training programme for a significant number of its support staff and managers. Training in community connecting was organized to run alongside additional training in person centred planning and this, in turn, was part of an explicit commitment to person centred working and supported living.

Initially, sixteen front line workers attended a two-day training event, which introduced them to the community connecting strategies, as outlined earlier in this book. The training included some theory in relation to community and friendship but focused particularly on the concept of giftedness as a key to unlocking potential connections. The course had a practical focus with an emphasis on tools of networking, community mapping, circles of support and brainstorming. Before coming on the course, these staff members had been asked to make an agreement with one service-user who was interested in increasing her social network. This ensured that people had someone in mind and had that person's agreement to try out some of the new strategies.

For six months after the initial training, the trainees came back on a monthly basis to discuss their progress, celebrate successes and support each other with problem-solving. The trainers who delivered the initial training facilitated these monthly peer-support meetings, but over time the group began to support each other without the need for a lot of direction.

The organization is keen to maximize the learning from this training and to continue to prioritise the peer-group discussion and support. Local networks are being set up for trainees to come together on a regular basis to discuss person centred working generally. An internal newsletter was produced specifically to spread the message about community connecting throughout the organization.

The community connecting work has been part of an ongoing evaluation. It has been evaluated on several levels to assess not only the outcomes for individual service-users, but also the outcomes for staff and projects within the organization.

Working effectively with family and friends

Community connecting should never be owned by agencies. To be successful it needs to include existing family and friends. Taking into account the individual's own wishes, family and friends need to be encouraged to be involved in the planning and the implementation of all community connecting initiatives.

In some instances relationships will have faded and will need to be rekindled. Sometimes community connecting will be as simple as supporting and strengthening existing relationships. Sometimes it will take no more than getting in touch with some people from the past who needed to be encouraged and supported back in. Sometimes the quickest way into community will be through the networks of family and friends as we saw in Chapter Five.

However, it is important to remember the conclusions of Wilmott's research on available natural support:

> Families with children or other members with severe disabilities may not be socially isolated, but they are likely to lack informal support of a sustained kind from outside the household.[105]

There will be a few instances when the individual is keen to distance themselves from existing family and friends and start anew. Obviously, their wishes need to be honoured.

Ultimately, agencies can only act as a catalyst. It is the family and friends who are there for the individual in the long term.

EVALUATION

As this is a new way of working, staff will be very conscious that there is a great deal of interest in what they are doing, at all levels of the system. Service users will be watching to see if this is something that they would like to request for themselves. Families and the organization will be watching to make sure that this is a valid use of staff time and resources. Service purchasers and commissioners will be interested to see how cost-effective this type of person centred service is.

Rather than be intimidated by this, it is important to set evaluation timescales and criteria. It is unfair to be expected to produce results immediately, but if there is a clear schedule for reporting and evaluating, this should alleviate everyone's stress.

The guiding principle behind any evaluation is that it should work for the specific context. Evaluation criteria need to relate to the organization and its service users, rather than be externally dictated. Any evaluation should:

- have measures that are defined by a range of stakeholders, including service users, family, front-line staff and managers
- allow for anecdotal telling of stories – this work cannot be measured in purely quantitative terms and this should be acknowledged from the start
- find things that can be measured and quantified – for example, complete a relationship map at the beginning and end of the work and see what changes have occurred
- seek to take account of changes at all levels – to the lives of service-users, to the role and attitude of staff and to the organization or project as a whole
- examine the affect on the community and its capacity to include people.

The individual, and those close to them, can undertake their own evaluation by defining criteria of success at the outset and measuring performance against them.[106] We may want to gain some objectivity and expertise from outsiders in which case we can:

- use staff from a different project within the organization
- employ an independent evaluator
- use staff who haven't directly been involved in the work
- set up a 'steering group' to guide the work of the evaluation team.

A word of caution

Some efforts promise friendship as an outcome of the application of certain strategies.

Uditsky argues convincingly that human services have long promised more than they can achieve and that friendship must be seen as more than '*a programmatic add-on*':

> It must be part of a broader values-based totality that calls for an inclusive community lifestyle, even when currently unachievable or extremely difficult. It is not enough to have friendship blocked . . . between menu planning and Special Olympics.[107]

Uditsky cautions human services against inventing new ways of fostering friendships. He advocates learning from community and providing opportunities rather than forcing a new agenda.

This pursuit of friendship formation knowledge must be employed with humility and not exalted as the latest human services reform ... Professionals run a risk in bringing human services friendship practices and assumptions into the community domain. It is incumbent upon them to be the students of friendship, not the masters. They can learn and teach more by example, by living lives that allow for friendship, than by the dissemination of any one method.[108]

This is not to say that human services are not obliged to support improvements in an individual's quality of life by supporting the development of friendships. But that human services should be allowing for opportunities for interaction between individuals and their community rather than dictating the path they should take.

This chapter has considered the implications of community connecting for organizations. We have viewed the matter from a number of different angles, focusing particularly on front-line staff, managers and organizations as a whole. We have also looked at a number of different organizations that all see community connecting as a core part of their service.

conclusion

When we first started training in community connecting, we stumbled on a quote about the search for communities in which relationships are based on mutuality rather than reciprocity. The meaning of this quote became clearer for us recently when we read a description of growing up on the Isle of Lewis:

> In the Hebridean vernacular economy, people understood themselves to be responsible for one another … At the deepest level of care is mutuality. As the owner of a fishing boat, let's say, I will give you fish simply because I have plenty and you have need. It would be nice if you could give me some eggs in return, but only if you're able so to do. If you can't because you are too sick, too old, or just a bit feckless, somebody else will see to it that I have eggs … Now, my giving you fish comes from a sense of obligation, because we are mutually part of the community. Likewise your giving me eggs. And nobody keeps a formal score of things because the village economy is centred around seeing that everybody has sufficient … Let's move on now to the second pillar of the vernacular economy: reciprocity. Here I catch the fish and you, let's say, still produce eggs. I agree to give you fish if you keep me in eggs … we measure only the function and not the degree of sharing. If the fishing is bad, you still give me eggs.[109]

What we have been attempting through this book is to find, build, and support communities that are based on mutuality as well as reciprocity – communities that we believe would work better for all of us.

Our search for community began with getting to know better, the individuals we were trying to connect. It continued by examining opportunities to connect within an individual's own networks and in our own. It broadened to look at how we could map communities and make better use of all the resources that are already available. And then went on to find ways in which we can all make

a contribution. The latter section of the book picked up on the changes that support staff, managers and organizations as a whole need to make in order to be effective in community connecting.

What we have found in our quest has been very encouraging:

- despite widely reported rumours of the death of community, it is still alive and well and there are numerous opportunities for people to join it
- much of the time, people are willing to help when asked to do something specific
- there are talented and committed community connectors working across the country, many of whom aren't even aware that they do it.

At the same time we discovered:

- the old truism that community connecting happens over time not overnight
- occasionally serendipitous incidences arise but most of the time community connecting requires strategic thinking and careful planning
- services are not dedicating enough time to this work, particularly given the huge difference it can make to the lives of the individuals they support
- purchasers do not see the value of the work and it is severely underfunded
- stories of successful community connecting are not being written up and used as evidence for funding the work
- there are not enough opportunities for people working in this area to learn from each other
- there is not enough evaluation of the effectiveness of different strategies for community connecting.

Our sense of the urgency and importance of this work was increased by the individuals, friends, family, and staff that we met during the course of our research. Many emphasised both the emptiness of some individual's lives and the difference it makes having people who care for you. This difference is not just a matter of happiness – being well-connected means that we are safer, more likely to get a job, more likely to be able to overcome difficulties in life and more likely to have a real sense of who we are and what contribution we can make to our world.

What ensues and emerges through connections and relationships can be exciting, messy, fulfilling, and frustrating, but at the root is being open and expectant to the spectacular vitality of life … [110]

appendix

Other windows

I. Communication

Many people either do not use words to talk or use few words. The communication section or 'window' is vital to developing an understanding about the individual. It needs to be completed very early in the development of the plan. Start it with the people who know the person best and then check it out with others. If the focus person lives with their family, they are usually the best people to begin this process with. Where a team supports the focus person, it is helpful to complete the section with it first. This window is useful . . .

- for exploring peoples' different perceptions about how the person communicates
- for explaining exactly how the person communicates with us.

In getting to know a person who does not use words to communicate, it is vital to find out how they communicate and to be aware of subtleties that are easily missed. It is important to find out who knows the person well and who is able to read the slight changes that can tell so much about how she is feeling. Listening to someone who does not use words means finding out:

- What are the person's mood indicators – how do we know if she is happy, sad, bored or angry, frustrated or excited in different settings, at different times. How do we gauge likes and dislikes?
- How does the person indicate choice or preference?
- How does the person use eye contact?
- What do other facial expressions mean? Are they obvious, like smiling, or something easier to miss?
- Do they use different vocal tones?
- When does the person fidget and when does she pay attention?
- What does her posture mean?

Any changes in how the individual engages or presents are important both for the outcome of the plan and informing the planning process.

There are many ways of recording the information gathered at this stage and often support from a Speech and Language Therapist, who is creative and experienced, will help a group to think through how best to make this information 'individual friendly' and accessible. These ways may involve photo-diaries, drawings, graphics and objects. Often it is necessary to try different ways

of recording before the most accessible is found. One way is the communication chart used in essential lifestyle planning. The communication chart is designed to support people who do not use words or have difficulty in communicating with words, to talk. It is also useful for people who do use words but whose speech is more difficult for others to understand.

At this time ...	Milly does this ...	We think it means...	We should ...
Anytime when you ask Milly a question	looks to the ceiling	yes	act accordingly
Anytime when you ask Milly a question	shakes her head	no	act accordingly
At anytime but particularly outside	repeatedly clenches her fingers	she's cold	cover her up ...
Anytime	puts her head down	she's unhappy	ask her directly what she's feeling

The communication chart has four headings.

- What is happening – describes the circumstances.
- (Person's name) does – describes what the person does in terms that are clear to a reader who has not seen it (a picture or even a video recording may be preferred for e.g., a facial expression).
- We think it means – describes the meaning that people think is behind the behaviour (it is not uncommon for there to be more than one meaning for a single behaviour – all meanings should be listed).
- And we should – describes what those who provide support are to do in response to what the person is saying with their behaviour (the responses under this heading give a careful reviewer a great deal of insight into how the person is perceived and supported.)

It is easiest to complete the communication chart by starting from the two inside columns first (when ... does, we think it means) and then working out to the two outside columns (what is happening, and we should). The most important thing to remember when compiling a communication chart is that the emphasis is on the appropriate response from those supporting the person, rather than on changing the behaviour

The communication chart may never be finished. It should be an ongoing process of recording and review and it can be used as a logbook with the aim of understanding and supporting the person in the best way possible.

2. History

A 'history' or past experiences window is useful:

- to keep in touch with the person's history
- to identify the landmark or milestone events in the person's life?
- to trace themes through a person's life story
- to identify experiences that must not be repeated
- to celebrate achievements
- to identify opportunities and positive experiences that can be built on
- to identify people or activities from the past that have gone missing and which the person might want to reintroduce.

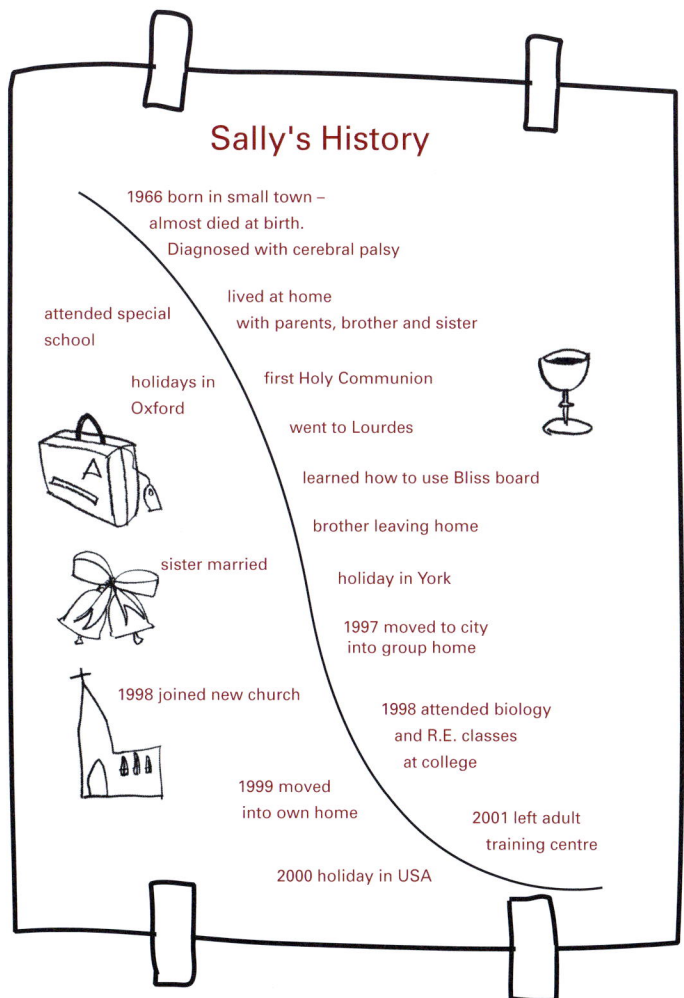

Sally's History

1966 born in small town – almost died at birth. Diagnosed with cerebral palsy

lived at home with parents, brother and sister

attended special school

holidays in Oxford

first Holy Communion

went to Lourdes

learned how to use Bliss board

brother leaving home

sister married

holiday in York

1997 moved to city into group home

1998 joined new church

1998 attended biology and R.E. classes at college

1999 moved into own home

2001 left adult training centre

2000 holiday in USA

3. Fears and nightmares

A fears and nightmares window is useful:

- to identify experiences to avoid at all cost
- to identify places to avoid
- to identify types of people to avoid
- for people to name their fears, especially if there is conflict over what is the right way forward for a person.

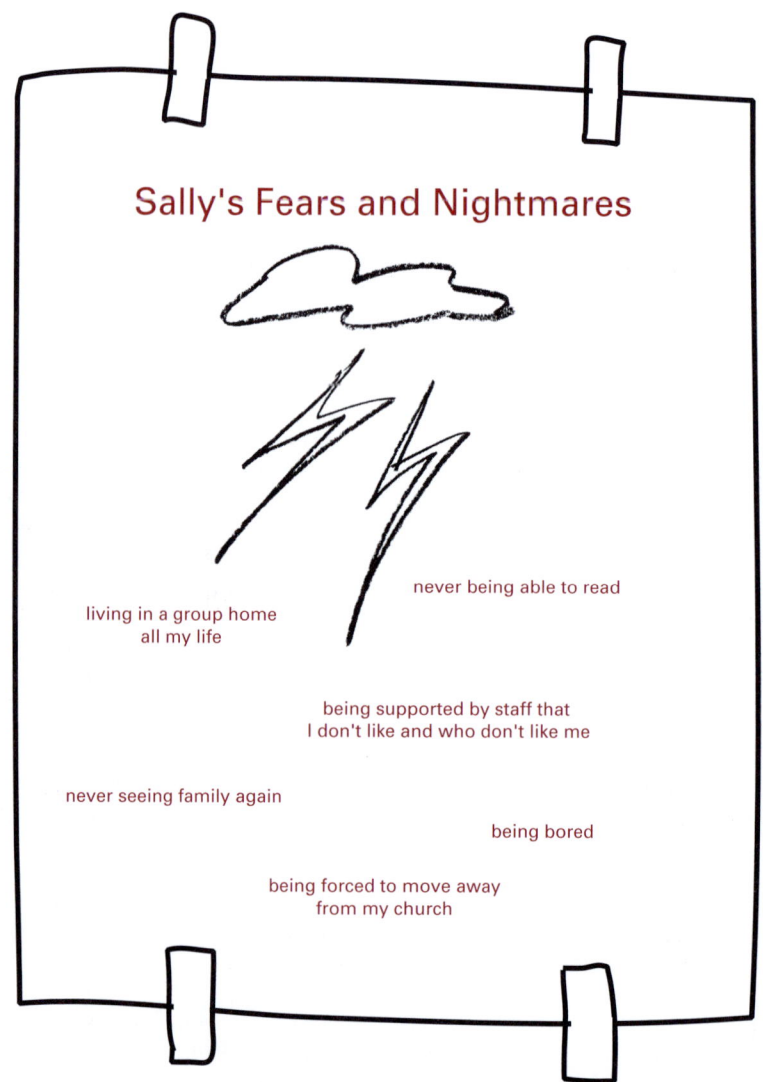

1   'Friendship: the Social Glue', Ray Pahl in *The Politics of Risk Society* ed Jane Franklin 1998 Policy Press

2   For instance the number of people with learning disabilities in hospital in Scotland has dropped from 6,430 in 1981 to 3,370 in 1994 and continues to drop (Scottish Office 1996)

3   Goffman, E., *Asylums*, Penguin, 1968

4   see Wolfensburger, 1972 and Kings fund, 1980

5   Oliver, 1990, cited in unpublished thesis by Chris Jones, 1998

6   Baldwin, 1993, cited in Jones, 1998

7   Lowe & Paiva, 1991, cited in Jones, 1998

8   Allen, 1989, cited in Jones, 1998

9   Jahoda et al, 1990; Simmons, 1991, cited in Jones, 1998

10 For example, in Alameda County in the USA, men and women who lacked ties to others were 1.9 to 3.1 times more likely to die in a 9 year follow-up period than people who had many more contacts. In addition there is some evidence that people who have supportive social networks are more infrequent users of health and social services in general … Social support is now generally accepted as having a beneficial effect on health and is important in changing the way people respond to stressful events and circumstances. Lack of a confiding relationship with a close friend, relative or partner is associated with poorer health, as is less involvement with wider social networks and community activities; see *On Your Doorstep*, Sainsbury Centre for Mental Health report.

11 Putnam, 2001

12 O'Briens, 1997

13 Wolfensburger, 1972

14 O'Brien, 1987

15 Sanderson et al., 1997

16 Kinsella, 1993

17 Oliver, 1990

18 Mary Hunt, 1991 cited in O'Briens, 1997

19 Communitas Inc. *Tending the Candle.*

20 And, more fully, in Wertheimer A., 1995

21 Tom Kohler

22 Kretzmann and McKnight

23 Deborah Reidy in Amado, 1993

24 Seymour Saranson, quoted in Schwartz, 1997

25 Kathy Bartholemew Lorimer cited in Amado, 1993

26 Jones C., 1998

27 Seymour Saranson, quoted in Schwartz, 1997

28 Ordinary Life Working Group (1988) *Ties and Connections.* London. King's Fund Centre.

29 O'Briens, 1997

30 Amado, 1993

31 ibid.

32 Heumann J (1993). 'A disabled woman's reflections: Myths and realities of integration', in J.Racino, P. Walker, S.O'Connor & S.Taylor, (eds) *Housing, support, and community: Choices and strategies for adults with disabilities.* Cambridge, MA: Brookline

33 French, 1994

34 Jones C., 1998

35 *Community Living*, January/February 2001. Jenny Barrett is Manager of The Elfrida Soceity's Supported Living Scheme Homelink.

36 Lutfiyya in Amado, 1993

37 Paraphrased from Betty Pendler in Amado, 1993

38 Cited in O'Briens, 1997

39 Perske and the O'Briens are cited in Amado, 1993

40 For more information on person centred planning see Sanderson et al., 1997

41 Mount, 1995

42 O'Briens, 1997

43 As defined by social service departments

44 There are several published formats that help people record their own information, such as 'Listen to me' or 'Thoughts about my Life', both based on essential lifestyle planning, and 'Capacity Works' and 'Life Building' based on Personal Futures Planning. These are tools for planning used by self-advocates, where the person either completes the information themselves or tells someone else what to write.

45 Smull and Sanderson, 2001

46 Duncan Yates personal communication

47 Personal Futures Planning is a tool to help clarify a path out of the stereotypes and programs that define and limit people. We enter each unique journey with people by weaving together the threads of a person's personal history and character, the contributions of the people who care for them, the opportunities and challenges in their local communities, and the resources in human service programmes. Personal Futures Planning is a process that helps design a road map for bringing these contributions into relationships and community life. Beth Mount. For more information cf. Sanderson et al., 1997

48 For a full description of essential lifestyle planning see Smull and Sanderson with Allen: 2001

49 Mount, 1995

50 O'Connell. M. (1988) *The gift of hospitality: Opening the doors of community life to people with disabilities.* p. 4 Evanston, IL: Center for Urban Affairs and Policy Research.

51 Amado, 1993

52 Snow: *What's Really Worth Doing and How to Do It*

53 Mount, 1995

54 Amado, 1993

55 Mount, 1995

56 Kathy Bartholemew-Lorimer

57 Reidy: 'Friendships and Community Associations', in Amado, 1993

58 Amado, 1993

59 Amado, 1993

60 Burton and Kagan, 1995

61 *The Same as You, A Review of Services for People with Support Needs.* Scottish Executive 2000. p. 78

62 Strully and Strully. 1993 as quoted in O'Briens, 1997

63 Cory Moore: Letting Go, Moving On. Amado. 1993

64 Cathy Busby: Richmond Fellowship Scotland describing one project's approach.

65 O'Briens, 1997

66 Oldenburg, 1989

67 Amado, 1993

68 O'Briens, 1997

69 Adapted from Kathryn Kemery McClain

70 McKnight, 1996

71 Schwartz, 1992

72 McKnight, 1996

73 Community builder at Options in Community Living.

74 Mount, 1995

75 Chambers English Dictionary

76 David Blunkett (*Analysis*, Radio 4 22 November 2001)

77 For more on volunteering see Bates P., *A Real Asset*, Manchester, National Development Team. 2002

78 For a variation on the LETS model see the chapter on Community Timebanks in *Working for Inclusion*, Bates (ed), Sainsbury Centre for Mental Health, 2002

79 LETSlink Scotland information leaflet

80 Ibid.

81 Glenn S. and Lyons C., (1996) *European Journal of Supported Employment and Vocational Rehabilitation*, Issue 2.

82 Jones et al. 1996

83 For this and Jenny's stories see *Women with Intellectual Disabilities*. Jessica Kingsley Publications, 2001

84 Nisbet J. and Hagner D., (1988) 'Natural supports in the workplace: a re-examination of supported employment', *Journal of the Association for Persons with Severe Handicaps*, 13, 260-267.

85 Jill is supported by Noble Centers, Inc, a nonprofit organization in Indianapolis and was part of the TASH Friendship Project research (1989-1991). For a more detailed account of this see Amado, 1993.

86 This and Stan's story were written by Duncan Yates.

87 Pat Beeman and George Ducharme

88 McKnight, 1996

89 Lord J and Pedlar A (1990) Life in the community: four years after the close of an institution. Kitchner, ON: Centre for Research and Education in Human Services. As quoted in *Members of Each Other*.

90 Amado, 1993

91 W. B. Yeats

92 Amado, 1993

93 McKnight J., 1996

94 Pete Ritchie, keynote address, Imagine Better, SHS Conference, 2000

95 There is also a section on how to evaluate inclusion in *Working for Inclusion*, P. Bates (ed.)

96 Carson D., (1994). 'Dangerous People: through a broader conception of risk and danger to better decisions', *Expert Evidence* 3(2) 51-69; quoted in 'Risking Legal Repercussions', in H.Kemshall and J.Pritchard (eds) (1996) *Good Practice in Risk Assessment and Risk Management 1*. London, Jessica Kingsley

97 Sanderson H., 2002. 'A plan is not enough: exploring the development of person centred teams', in *Person Centred Planning, Research, Practice and Future Directions*. Steve Holburn and Peter M. Vietze (eds.) Paul H. Brookes. Baltimore.

98 Ritchie, P, *Community Connecting and Person Centred Planning*, 2001. Unpublished paper

99 Quoted in Amado, 1993

100 See Will in the previous chapter who only needs 1 to 1 support when he is at work.

101 Inclusion Alliance

102 Amado, 1993

103 *Steps for Supporting Community Connections.* Amado, 1993

104 Amado, 1993

105 Wilmott P. (1987) *Friendship Networks and Social Support.* PSI Research Report No.666. London, Policy Studies Institute

106 For ways of undertaking evaluation in this way see *Achieving Better Community Development* and *Learning, Evaluation and Planning* published by the Community Development Foundation, London

107 Uditsky in Amado, 1993

108 Ibid

109 McIntosh, 2002

110 Sousa M. E., (1991, December) Report to the TASH Friendship Project Director

Allen D., *The effects of deinstitutionalisation on people with mental handicaps: a review*, Mental Handicap Research, 2, 1989, pp. 18-37.

Amado, A., Conkin, F. & Wells, J., *Friends: A manual for connecting persons with disabilities and community members*, Minnesota, Governor's Planning Council on Developmental Disabilities

Amado, A., *Friendships and Community Connections between People with and without Developmental Disabilities*, Paul Brookes Publishing, 1993

Baldwin S., , *The Myth of Community Care: An alternative neighbourhood model of care*, Chapman & Hall, London, 1993

Barnes, C. (ed.), *Making Our Own Choices*, British Council of Organizations of Disabled People, Coventry, 1992

Barr, A. & Hashagen, S., *Achieving Better Community Development*, Community Development Foundation, London, 2000

Bates, P. (ed), *Working for Inclusion*, The Sainsbury Centre for Mental Health.,2002

Bates, P., *A Real Asset*, Manchester. National Development Team, 2002.

Bradley, V., Ashbaugh, J. and Blaney, B., (eds) *Benefits and Limitations of Personal Futures Planning in Creating Individual Supports for People with Developmental Disabilities – A Mandate for Change at Many Levels*, Paul H Brookes Publishing, Baltimore, 1994

Brost, M., Johnson, T. Z. & Deprey, R. K., *Getting to Know You: One Approach to Service Planning and Assessment for People with Learning Difficulties*, Wisconsin Coalition for Advocacy, Madison WI, 1982

Burton, M. and Kagan, C. with Clements, P., *Social Skills for People with Learning Difficulties*, Chapman and Hall, London, 1995

Communitas Inc., *One Candle Power: Building Bridges into Community Life for People with Disabilities*, Communitas, Inc., Connecticut

Communitas Inc. *Tending the Candle*, Communitas Inc. Connecticut

Communitas Inc., *What are We Learning About Bridge-Building? A Summary of a Dialogue Between People Seeking to Build Community for People with Disabilities.* Communitas, Inc., Connecticut

Communitas Inc., *Dare to Dream: An Analysis of the Conditions Leading to Personal Change for People with Disabilities*, Communitas Inc., Connecticut

Communitas Inc., *Imperfect Change: Embracing the Tensions of Person-Centred Work Person Centred Development: A Journey in Learning to Listen to People with Disabilities*, Communitas Inc., Connecticut

Curtis, E. & Dezelsky, M., *A Self-determined Life: Tools to support dignity, diversity, community and dreams*, New Hats Inc., USA

Falvey, M., Forest, M., Pearpoint, J. & Rosenberg, R., (1993) *All My Life's a Circle*, Inclusion Press Toronto, 1993 (available from Inclusion Press, UK Distribution)

Finkelstein, V., Oliver, M. & Swain, J., *Disabling Barriers-Enabling Environments*, Sage, London, 1993

Forest, M., O'Brien, J. & Pearpoint, J., *PATH: A Workbook for Planning Positive, Possible Futures*, Inclusion Press, Toronto (available from Inclusion Press UK Distribution)

Forest, M., & Pearpoint, J., *The Inclusion Process - Strategies to Make Inclusion Work*, Inclusion Press, Toronto (available from Inclusion Press UK Distribution)

Franklin, J. (ed), *The Politics of a Risk Society*, Policy Press, 1998

Glover, J., *The Philosophy & Psychology of Personal Identity*, Penguin, London, 1988

French S., 'Institutional and community living', in: French, S. (ed.), *On Equal Terms: Working with Disabled People*, Butterworth Heinemann, Oxford, 1994

Goffman, E., *Asylums*. Penguin, 1961

Galambos, D., *Planning to Have a Life*, Sheridan College, Ontario, 1996

Goodley, D., *Self Advocacy in the Lives of People with Learning Difficulties*, OUP, 2000

Handy, C., *The Age of Unreason*, Arrow Books, USA, 1985

Handy, C., (1978) The Gods of Management. USA: Century Business

Inclusion Press, (ed.), Inclusion News. Toronto: Inclusion Press (available from Inclusion Press UK Distribution)

Jahoda, A., Cattermole, M. & Markova, I., 'Moving Out: An opportunity for friendship and broadening social horizons?', *Journal of Mental Deficiency Research. 34*, 1990, pp. 127-39.

Jones, C., *The Meaning of Community Care for People with Learning Difficulties and Paid Support Staff*, unpublished MSc thesis, 1998

Jones, C., Ritchie, P. & Broderick, L., *Ways to Work: Converting Day Services*, SHS Ltd, Edinburgh, 1996

Kagan, C. & Rall, D., *Participation in and by communities: What can we learn from Community Development?*, North West Training and Development Team, UK

Kennedy, J., Munro, K., Ritchie, P., Smith, A. and Wilson, H., *Community Living – Implications for People and Agencies*, Scottish Human Services Trust, Edinburgh, 1997

King's Fund, *An Ordinary Life: comprehensive locally-based residential services for mentally handicapped people*, King's Fund, London, 1980

Kinsella, P., *Supported Living - A New Paradigm*, NDT, Manchester, 1993

Kinsella, P. & Goodwin, G., *Guidebook for Evaluation Teams*, Liverpool Health Authority internal document, 1996

Kretzmann, J., & McKnight, J., *Building Communities from the Inside Out: A path toward finding and mobilizing a community's assets*, ACTA Publications, Chicago,

Lowe K. & Paiva S., 'Clients' community and social contacts: results of a five year longitudinal study', *Journal of Mental Deficiency Research*. 35, 1991, pp. 308-323.

Lovett, H., *Learning to Listen*, Jessica Kingsley, London, 1996

McIntosh, A., *Soil and Soul: People Versus Corporate Power*, Aurum Press, 2002

McKnight, J., *The Careless Society*, Basic Books, USA, 1996

Mental Health Foundation, *Building Expectations: Opportunities and Services for People with a Learning Disability*, The Mental Health Foundation, London, 1996

Mount, B., (1995), *Capacity Works: Finding Windows for Change Using Personal Futures Planning*, Communitas, Inc., Connecticut, 1995

Mount, B., Beeman, P., Ducharme, G., *What are we Learning About Circles of Support? A Collection of Tools, Ideas and Reflections on Building and Facilitating Circles of Support*, Communitas, Inc., Connecticut

Mount, B., *Capacity Works*, Capacity Works, 1995

Mount, B. *Life Building: Opening Windows to Change Using Personal Futures Planning Personal Workbook*, Capacity Works, 2000

Murray, P. & Penman, J., *Let our Children Be*, Parents with Attitude, Sheffield, 1996

New Hats Inc., *I want my Dream Deck, Hat Cards and Profiles Deck*, New Hats Inc., USA

O'Brien, J., *A Framework for Accomplishment*, Responsive Systems Associates, Decatur USC, 1987

O'Brien, J., *Learning From Citizen Advocacy Programs*, Georgia Advocacy Office

O'Brien, J. & Lovett, H., *Finding a Way Toward Everyday Lives: The Contribution of Person centred Planning*, Pennsylvania Office of Mental Retardation, Harrisburg, Pennsylvania, 1992

O'Brien, J. & O'Brien, C.L., *More Than Just a New Address: Images of Organization for Supported Living Agencies, Responsive Systems Associates*, Lithonia, 1991

O'Brien, J. & O'Brien, C.L., (eds.), *Remembering the Soul of Our Work: Stories by the Staff of Options in Community Living*, Options in Community Living, Madison, 1992

O'Brien, J., & O'Brien, C.L., *Members of Each Other*, Inclusion Press, Toronto, 1997 (available from Inclusion Press UK Distribution)

O'Brien, J., O'Brien, C.L. & Schwartz, D. B., (eds), *What Can We Count On to Make and Keep People Safe?*. Lithonia: Responsive Systems Associates, 1990

Oldenburg, R., *The Great Good Place: Cafes, Coffee Shops, Community Centers, Beauty Parlors, General Stores, Hangouts and how they get you through the day*, Paragon, New York, 1989

Oliver, M., The Politics of Disablement. Basingstoke, MacMillan Press, 1990

Oliver, M., *Understanding Disability: From theory to practice*, MacMillan, 1996

Ordinary Life Working Group, *Ties and Connections*, Kings Fund Centre, London, 1988

Pearpoint, J., O'Brien, J., & Forest, M., *PATH: A Workbook for Planning Positive Possible Futures*, Inclusion Press Toronto (available from Inclusion Press UK Distribution)

People First Liverpool and Manchester, *Our Plan for Planning*, People First, Manchester, 1996

Putnam, R.D., *Bowling Alone: The Collapse and Revival of American Community*, Simon and Schuster, 2000

Racino, J., Walker, P., O'Connor, S. & Taylor, S., *Housing, Support and Community: Choices and Strategies for Adults with Disabilities*, Paul H. Brookes Publishing Co., Maryland, 1993

Sanderson, H., Kennedy, J. & Ritchie, P., *People Plans and Possibilities*, Scottish Human Services Trust. 1997

Schleien, Stuart J., Tipton Ray, M., & Green, F.P., *Community Recreation and People with Disabilities: Strategies for Inclusion,* Paul H.Brookes Publishing Company, 1997

Schwartz, D., (1992), *Crossing the River: Creating a Conceptual Revolution in Community and Disability*, Brookline Books, USA, 1992 (UK distributor: Values Incorporated)

Schwartz, D., *Who Cares? Rediscovering Community*, Westview Press USA, 1997 (UK distributor: Values Incorporated)

The Same as You. A Review of Services for People with Learning Disabilities, Scottish Executive 2000

The Sainsbury Centre for Mental Health, *On Your Doorstep. Community Organisations and Mental Health*, The Sainsbury Centre for Mental Health, London, 2000

Smale, G. & Tuson, G., *Empowerment, Assessment, Care Management and the Skilled Worker*, HMSO, London, 1993

Smull, M., *Increasing Quality While Reducing Costs: The Challenge of the 1990's in Creating Individual Supports for People with Developmental Disabilities – A Mandate for Change at Many Levels*, Baltimore, 1994

Smull, M., & Burke-Harrison, S., *Supporting People with Severe Reputations in the Community*, National Association of State Directors of Developmental Disabilities Services Inc., Virginia, 1992

Smull, M & Sanderson, H., *Essential Lifestyle Planning – a handbook for facilitators, North West Training and Development Team*, Manchester, 2001

Snow, J., *What's Really Worth Doing and How to Do It*, Inclusion Press, Toronto

Stalker, K., & Campbell, V., *Person Centred Planning: An Evaluation of a Training Programme*, Stirling University Social Work Research Centre, Stirling, 1996

Towell, D., *Person Centred Planning: The Implications for Organisational Development in the Mixed Economy of Welfare – Notes on a King's Fund College / NDT Workshop*, King's Fund College, London, 1993

Traustadottir, R. & Johnson, K. (eds.) *Women with Intellectual Disabilities*, Jessica Kingsley, 2000

Wertheimer, A., (ed.), *Circles of Support: Building Inclusive Communities*, available from Circles Network, Bristol, 1995

Wetherow, D., (ed.), *The Whole Community Catalogue*, Gunnars and Campbell Publishers Inc., USA

Wolfensberger, W., *The Principle of Normalization in Human Services*, National Institute on Mental Retardation, Toronto, 1972

Wolfensberger, W., & Glenn, S., (1975), *PASS: Program Analysis of Service Systems. Handbook and Field Manual* (3rd edition), National Institute on Mental Retardation, Toronto, 1975

Wolfensberger, W., & Thomas, S., *PASSING: Program Analysis of Service Implementation Goals*, National Institute on Mental Retardation, Toronto, 1983

Zarb, G., & Nadash, P., *Cashing In on Independence*, British Council of Organizations of Disabled People, Derby, 1994